PREFACE:

Welcome to the fan's guide from A to Z! It was really fun compiling this book, and I enjoyed learning new things about the Nationals, and baseball, in the process. Here is how things are organized and presented:

You can locate what interests you either by letter section or by consulting the index in the back. Be aware I had to juggle things around so I would have some balance under the letters. For example, I put most of the strikeout stats under "K." Desperate for something for "V," I headed WAR under "Value Statistics." "No Hitter" and "Shutouts" were placed under "Z" for "zeroes," another challenging letter! I hope this does not cause consternation or confusion as you try to find a category. There is also an appendix at the end listing various stats—both good and bad.

Highlighting and colors are used many times to maybe give the text more of a "pop." In the cases of most stat lists, I note that the ranked 1-2-3 players are highlighted.

The book covers the Nationals 2005-15. I have included some background and history on the Expos and D.C. baseball.

In "FUN FACTS," I have included MLB leaders in that category and some history of baseball. I hope you enjoy that. One of my favorite things is to read about "old time" baseball and I highly recommend such fantastic books as *The Glory of Their Times* by Lawrence S. Ritter (the audiobook is great), *Crazy Eights* by Cait N. Murphy, *Eight Men Out* by Eliot Asinof, *Ty and the Babe* by Tom Stanton, and *The Gas House Gang* by John Heidenry.

Thank you to fangraphs.com, mlb.com, baseballreference.com, and baseball-almanac.com for the great information available. I tried hard to double and triple check stats and info, and apologize if there are any errors or discrepancies. I have cited the source of stats that are more complicated and seem to differ from site to site.

I hope you enjoy the book!

Ann Lambert Good
Great Falls, Virginia

www.mascotbooks.com

Washington Nationals A to Z

For more information, please contact:
Mascot Books
560 Herndon Parkway #120
Herndon, VA 20170
info@mascotbooks.com

Library of Congress Control Number: 2016905820

CPSIA Code: PBANG0516A
ISBN-13: 978-1-63177-624-3

Printed in the United States

Washington Nationals A TO Z

BY ANN LAMBERT GOOD

(Photos: Courtesy of Steve Good)

INTRODUCTION:

Washington Nationals—The History

In 2005, after thirty-four long years, baseball finally returned to Washington, D.C. with the Montreal Expos (the first team in Canada) making the move to become the Washington Nationals. This was the first move of an MLB franchise since the second Senators franchise left D.C. for Arlington, Texas, in 1971 (the last NL team to move was the Braves from Milwaukee to Atlanta after the 1965 season).

It was obviously a long time coming. There were obstacles along the way. First, there was the claim that D.C. was not a "true baseball town," having lost the Senators not once, but twice. Also, the Baltimore Orioles owners claimed that the market already had a team, meaning that D.C. would not be able to sustain a new franchise (similar to the first item). Further complicating the effort is the D.C. market, which encompasses 3 different jurisdictions (DC/VA/MD), making everything more difficult.

Even once MLB had committed to moving the Expos to D.C., there were a number of issues to get through, including getting the agreement of the Baltimore Orioles owner (focusing on broadcasting rights), making a decision about the location for the D.C. team (there was a strong pitch by a Virginia group to put the new stadium in VA), and figuring out how to finance the move. It became a big political issue for D.C. on getting City Council approval for the financing portion of the new $581 million stadium (without support from VA or MD; again, the three-in-one market issue). MLB pitched in with some money, and D.C. was finally able to arrange financing for the new Nationals Park.

Once the D.C. location was firmed up by MLB, the plan was to have the new team play three years at RFK (home of the Senators for ten years), while a new stadium was built along the Anacostia River waterfront, where Nationals Park is indeed located and opened in 2008.

At the time of the move in 2005, MLB owned the Expos. This evolved because the Expos, originally earmarked for contracting after the 2001 season, instead shifted to ownership by the other 29 MLB owners on February 15, 2002, an arrangement due to expire in December 2006. MLB purchased the Expos for $120 million from Jeffrey Loria and his minority partners. It was on September 29, 2004 that MLB announced that the Expos would move to Washington, D.C. in 2005. The Lerner Enterprise Group was finally selected by MLB as the new owners in July 2006.

How was the name selected? There was extensive discussion about (and strong support for) reviving the "Senators," but the Texas Rangers still owned the rights to the name, and some D.C. politicians opposed this name because the District of Columbia does not indeed have a Senator or voting representation in Congress. Also, the original Senators had some glory years (Walter Johnson, etc.), but the most recent Senators franchise was remembered as a losing team. D.C. mayor Anthony A. Williams supported the name "Washington Grays" after the Negro League team, the Homestead Grays (192950), which played half of their home games in Washington from 194042, but was actually based in Pittsburgh. According to the Washington Post, MLB used focus groups of Washingtonians to help inform their selection process for a new franchise name. On September 30, 2004, the Washington Post included the following suggested names in their "Name the Team" survey:

Bandits/Beltway Bandits
Bullets
Cicadas
Federals
Filibusters
Expos
Grays
Monuments
Nationals
Patriots
Senators
Snakeheads
River Rats/Dogs

Were some of those choices serious? As for the selection of "Nationals" for the new team, it shares a deep history in D.C., closely connected with the Senators. Way back in 1859, Washington had two teams called the Nationals and the Potomacs. The Senators team established by the new American League in 1901 officially changed their name to the Nationals in 1905. Senators and Nationals were both used in the newspapers until 1957, when owner Clark Griffith changed the name to Senators. Those Senators left for Minnesota after the 1960 season, but the expansion team that replaced it took on the Senators name. This second Senators team, headed at the end by HOFer Ted Williams, moved to Texas after the 1971 season.

On November 23, 2004, team president Tony Tavares and D.C. Mayor Williams unveiled the new "Washington Nationals" team name and logo in a ceremony at Union Station. Williams, Tavares, and General Manager Jim Bowden donned red hats adorned with a script "W," replicas of the Senators hats worn from 196271.

Baseball finally returned to D.C. on April 14, 2005 when President George W. Bush, looking sporty in a Nats jacket, threw out an energetic ceremonial first pitch, about shoulder-high, to Nats catcher Brian Schneider. Former Senators were then announced as they headed out to their old positions, including Frank Howard, Roy Sievers and Ed Brinkman. Livan Hernandez took the mound and pitched 8 shutout innings for the Nats, and they beat the Arizona Diamondbacks 53 under the leadership of HOF manager Frank Robinson. One write-up on the first home game (spamomatic.org) included some of the player walkup songs that night (50 Cent was very popular):

- Nick Johnson (1B): Snoop Dogg's "Drop it Like it's Hot" and 50 Cent's "Hate It or Love It"

- Jose Vidro (2B): Montell Jordan's "This is How We Do It"

- Jose Guillen (RF): A song by 50 Cent

- Ryan Church (CF): 50 Cent and Lil' Kim's "Magic Stick" and John Fogerty's "Fortunate Son"

- Vinny Castilla (3B): Ciara and Petey Pablo's "Goodies" and 50 Cent's "In Da Club"

- Brian Schneider (C) and Brad Wilkerson (LF): unidentified techno

- Cristian Guzman (SS): a GUnit song

Another important music note: 2005 saw the introduction of Chuck Brown's "Bustin' Loose" song after Nats home runs; in 2008, for the new stadium, Nats fans voted to keep this tradition.

So the 2005 Nats ended up 8181, a .500 winning percentage, in last place in the National League East (NLEast), but were #1 among all NL teams in interleague play, recording 12 wins (always looking for the good news). In 2006, the Nats lost ground, going 7191, but the season featured the first Beltway Series matchup against the Baltimore Orioles. Each team won two games at home and one on the road for a 33 tie. 2007 was the final year at RFK, and the Nats moved up in the NLEast standings to 4th place, even though they lost ground a bit on wins (7389). This year saw the first player award for the Nats when Dmitri Young won MLB Comeback Player of the Year; he was also the team representative to the All-Star Game. Looking to the future, RHP Jordan Zimmermann was drafted in June 2007. The Nats had good and bad news in 2008. First, the bad news was finishing 59102 with the worst record in MLB, and last in the NLEast. The good news was that they moved into beautiful Nationals Park. Looking to the future, Danny Espinosa and Tyler Moore were drafted in June 2008.

So, 2009 was a tiny bit worse than 2008 with the Nats' 59103 record (last in the division). That year, the interlocking "D.C." was removed from the star-spangled circle on caps and replaced by the curly "W." It felt like the team reached a new low when Ryan Zimmerman and Adam Dunn showed up with jerseys reading "Natinals," which would have been funnier if the team had been doing better at the time. The new slim version of mascot "Screech" was introduced that year--some of us missed the old Screech, but got used to the new one after a while. And 2009 was the year that the Nats selected Stephen Strasburg as the first pick overall in the draft. In 2010, we saw progress with a 6983 record (10 more wins!), but this still meant last place in the NLEast for a third year in a row. Yet this was the year of "Strasmas" when Strasburg made his exciting debut with 14 strikeouts on June 8 against the Miami Marlins. Ryan Zimmerman won a Silver Slugger award for 3rd base the second year in a row. And, it was in 2010 that the Nats selected Bryce Harper first pick overall in the draft.

2011 was a turnaround year; the Nats finished third in the NL East, getting almost back to .500 with 80 wins, 81 losses (.497) (only 161 games due to a rainout versus the Dodgers). This was the Nats' best finish to date in the standings (second best in terms of winning percentage—2005 was better). Anthony Rendon was drafted by the Nats in June 2011 (sixth pick overall). In 2012, the Nats moved on and up to clinch the NLEast with a 9864 record. Needless to say, this was a very exciting year for the Nationals, led by Manager Davey Johnson, who won the NL Manager of the Year award. In the first round of the playoffs, the Nats looked so promising, but ultimately succumbed to the St. Louis Cardinals in game five. The first ever playoffs were amazingly exciting for the Nats fans nonetheless.

In 2013, there was a bit of slippage to 2nd place in the NL East (8676 record), with the Braves coming in 1st; this was our second largest attendance year to date (2005 had the highest attendance). Bryce Harper and Jordan Zimmermann were selected as All-Stars and Michael Morse left for the Mariners; A.J. Cole and Blake Treinen came in from the Athletics. 2014 was better, and the Nats ended up in 1st place again (9666), this time with the best record in the overall NL. The loss in four games to the Giants was heartbreaking (see longest game below), because there was a lot of hope of going all the way. Manager Matt Williams was named NL Manager of the Year, Anthony Rendon won the Silver Slugger Award for 3B in his first full season, and Wilson Ramos received the 2014 Tony Conigliaro Award for the courage he displayed in overcoming his 2011 kidnapping in Venezuela.

So 2015 was kind of an exhausting year; expectations were extremely high, but the frustration with our win/loss record was offset by the amazing seasons of both Bryce Harper and new Nats pitcher, Max Scherzer (take a look at their accomplishments below). It was a surprise that so many of our starting players were out due to injuries, and the Nats ended up in 2nd place with an 8379 record. During the season, the Nats gained some notoriety for their painful "slow jams" played during the visiting team's batting practice (really an odd experience for the uninformed who happened to show up early).

In contrast to the walkup songs players selected in 2005, here are some of the 2015 Nats selections:

- Bryce Harper (RF): "The Best is Yet to Come" by Frank Sinatra, "Flower" by Moby

- Jayson Werth (LF): "Werewolves of London" by Warren Zevon, "Rains of Castamere" by The National for Game of Thrones

- Wilson Ramos (C): "Wilson" by Phish

- Jordan Zimmermann (P): "Hell on Wheels" by Brantley Gilbert, "Son's Gonna Rise" by Citizen Cope

- Danny Espinosa (2B): "Simple Man" by Lynyrd Skynyrd

- Ian Desmond (SS): "Alright" by Kendrick Lamar

- Max Scherzer (P): "Energy" by Drake, "Going Down For Real" by Flo Rida

- Ryan Zimmerman (1B): "Lazaretto" by Jack White

- Stephen Strasburg (P): "Seven Nation Army" by The White Stripes

- Anthony Rendon (3B): "No Competition" by Bun B

Looking forward to an exciting 2016 season!

A *is for...*

Nats **A**ll-Stars:

2005: Chad Cordero P, Livan Hernandez P

The first ever Nats All-Stars! Hernandez pitched one inning; Cordero entered the bottom of the eighth with two outs and struck out Ivan Rodriguez (future NAT).

2006: Alfonso Soriano LF

The third player in MLB history to start an All-Star Game in both leagues at two different positions (LF for NL, and 2B for AL). Soriano singled in the third and stole 2B.

2007: Dmitri Young 1B

As DH, Young had a ground ball single in the bottom of the 9th and scored on Alfonso Soriano's (then with the Chicago cubs) home run. Late rally could not overcome the deficit, and NL lost 5 4.

2008: Cristian Guzman SS

Guzman entered as a pinch runner in the top of the 9th, was caught stealing. The SS played 3rd base in the game, went 0 for 3.

2009: Ryan Zimmerman 3B

Zimmerman entered in the bottom of the 5TH at 3B, went 0 for 2.

2010: Matt Capps P

Capps entered in the bottom of the 6th, got David Ortiz to strike out looking. Capps got the win (3-1), ending a 13 year NL drought at the All-Star Game.

2011: Tyler Clippard P

Clippard was the second Nat in a row to get the win in the All-Star Game. He was also the first pitcher in MLB history to earn a win in an All-Star or postseason game by facing only one batter and allowing a hit. Adrian Beltre singled off Clippard in the top of the 4th but Hunter Pence threw out the runner at home plate.

2012: Ian Desmond SS, Gio Gonzalez P, Bryce Harper OF, Stephen Strasburg P

Gonzalez and Strasburg each pitched scoreless innings; Gonzalez in the third facing three batters, and Strasburg in the fourth facing four. Harper entered as a PH for Carlos Beltran in the 5th, played LF, went 0 for 1. Harper, age 19, was the third youngest player ever elected to the All-Star Game, after Dwight Gooden and Bob Feller, and the youngest ever position player (Gooden and Feller being pitchers). Desmond had to withdraw due to injury (left oblique strain).

2013: Bryce Harper OF, Jordan Zimmermann P

In his second All-Star game and as a starter this time, Harper had two catches in center, went 0 for 2 and exited in the 6th. He became the youngest NL starter in All-Star game history. He was the second Nat after Soriano to start. Zimmermann could not play due to stiffness in the neck.

2013 Home Run Derby

Harper made it to the final round, with his father pitching to him and sporting an impressive mohawk, and ended up coming in 2nd to Yoenis Cespedes (9 to 8). Harper was the second youngest player to compete in the Derby, being older than Ken Griffey Jr. in his 1990 appearance by only 39 days. He became the first (and so far only) Nat to compete in the Derby.

2014: Tyler Clippard P, Jordan Zimmermann P

Clippard faced two batters—Jose Altuve and Miquel Cabrera—in the 5th inning, throwing 11 pitches (8 strikes), and did not give up a hit. Zimmermann unfortunately had to sit out his second Midsummer Classic due to injury.

2015: Bryce Harper OF, Max Scherzer P

Bryce Harper was the leading vote getter in 2015, with 13,964,950 fan votes, the most of any player to appear on the NL ballot. Max Scherzer had to decline participation due to where the game fell on his pitching schedule. Harper played RF and went 0 for 3 with two strikeouts.

At Nationals Park In 2018

THE NATIONALS WILL BE HOSTING THE ALL-STAR GAME IN 2018.

Fun Fact: The first All-Star Game was in 1933 at the Chicago White Sox's Comiskey Park. Cleveland Stadium and Old Yankee Stadium are tied for the most times a stadium has hosted the game, with four each. The Nats and the Tampa Bay Rays are the only teams that have not hosted the Classic.

Another Fun Fact: The first Home Run Derby was in 1985 at Minneapolis; it was then a contest between leagues (5 players each) and the AL won 17-16. In Derby history, Ken Griffey, Jr. CF (Mariners/Reds) has the most wins (3) and most appearances (8). Josh Hamilton OF (Rangers) hit the most HRs in one round (18—2008), and Bobby Abreu RF (Phillies) the most overall HRs in one event (41-2005).

Year	Venue	Attendance
1937	Griffith Stadium	31,391
1956	Griffith Stadium	28,843
1962	D.C. (RFK) Stadium	45,480
1969	RFK Stadium	45,259

***The Montreal EXPOS hosted the Summer Classic once, in 1982.*

Highlights Of D.C. All-Star Games:

1937: The first pitch was thrown by President Franklin D. Roosevelt, and ended in an AL victory 8-3 over the NL. Dizzy Dean (Cardinals) and Lefty Gomez (Yankees) were the starting pitchers; during the game Dizzy Dean's toe was broken when he was struck by an Earl Averill (Indians) hit. Senator All-Stars: Rick Ferrell (C), Wes Ferrell (P). Wes and Rick were brothers and teammates from 1933-37; they both played in the 1933 and 1937 All-Star games. Rick was elected to the HOF by the Veterans Committee in 1984.

1956: The game featured home runs by Willie Mays and Stan Musial for the NL, and Mickey Mantle and Ted Williams for the AL. Starting pitchers were Billy Pierce (Chicago White Sox) and Bob Friend (Pittsburgh Pirates); NL won 7-3 with Friend earning the win, and Johnny Antonelli (San Francisco Giants) got the save. Senator All-Stars: Roy Sievers (OF). Sievers was a five-time All-Star, AL Rookie of the Year (1949), AL home run and RBI champion (1957).

1962: President John F. Kennedy threw out the first pitch, and the NL won 3-1. Maury Wills of the Los Angeles Dodgers was the MVP. Starting pitchers were Don Drysdale (Dodgers), and Jim Bunning (Tigers); Juan Marichal (San Francisco Giants) got the win. Senator All-Stars: Dave Stenhouse (P). Stenhouse, a rookie at the time, was selected as the starting pitcher for the OTHER 1962 All-Star Game at Wrigley Field, against Johnny Podres (Dodgers).

Fun Fact: The 1962 game was one of two (July 10th in D.C. and the other July 30th at Wrigley Field) All-Star Games because from 1959-62 a second game was added to raise money for the MLB players' pension funds, as well as other causes. This was abandoned because having two games watered down the appeal and impact of the event.

1969: The 40th All-Star Game resulted in a 9-3 victory for the NL. The original date of July 22nd was rained out, so the game took place on July 23rd. Senator All-Stars: starter Frank Howard (OF), and Darold Knowles (LHP). Per Wikipedia, Knowles is the only pitcher to have played in all 7 games of a World Series (1973 with the Oakland Athletics). Howard ("Hondo") was a two-time AL home run champion (1968 and 1970) and AL RBI champion (1970) with the Senators.

Attendance At Nats Games

Top 5 Games (5 games with largest attendance)

1. 45,966—NLDS Game 5, Friday, October 12, 2012—vs Cardinals: It was better to attend game 4 when Jayson Werth hit the amazing walk off home run. This was the sad ending to the Nats playoffs, with a loss 9-7 to the Cardinals on a cold fall night.

2. 45,596—2005 Regular Season Game #10 on April 14, 2005— Opening Day Inaugural Season 2005 at RFK vs Arizona: Such an exciting day at RFK with Livan Hernandez pitching eight shutout innings and Chad Cordero recording the save in a 5-3 win over the Arizona Diamondbacks.

3. 45,274—2013 Regular Season Game #1 on April 1, 2013— Opening Day at Nationals Park vs Marlins: The excitement carrying over from the 2012 postseason experience, Strasburg got the win over the Marlins, 2-0.

4. 44,685—2011 Regular Season Game #124 on August 20, 2011— vs Philadelphia: A large crowd, unfortunately filled with a significant number of Phillies fans (who came to boo Jayson Werth) witnessed a Phillies shutout of the Nats, 5-0 (W Oswalt, L Lannan).

5. 44,492—2005 Regular Season Game #85 at RFK on July 7, 2005— vs Mets: Eleven inning loss to the Mets, 3-2; Tony Armas started and Luis Ayala took the loss.

2005	2,731,993 (#11) (33,728)	#1 Yankees 4,090,696 (50,502)
2006	2,153,056 (#21) (26,580)	#1 Yankees 4,248,067 (52,392)
2007	1,943,812 (#25) (24,217)	#1 Yankees 4,171,083 (52,729)
2008	2,320,400 (#20) (29,005)	#1 Yankees 4,298,655 (53,069)
2009	1,817,226 (#24) (22,715)	#1 Dodgers 3,761,655 (46.440)
2010	1,828,066 (#23) (22,568)	#1 Phillies 3,777,322 (46,491)
2011	1,940,478 (#21) (24,877)	#1 Phillies 3,680,718 (45,440)
2012	2,370,794 (#15) (30,010)	#1 Phillies 3,565,718 (44,021)
2013	2,652,422 (#11) (32,745)	#1 Dodgers 3,743,527 (46,216)
2014	2,579,389 (#12) (31,844)	#1 Dodgers 3,782,337 (46,695)
2015	2,619,843 (#11) (32,343)	#1 Dodgers 3,764,815 (46,479)

Fun Fact: You may be wondering: how many attended on STRASMAS Day? On Tuesday, June 8, 2010 (Game #59), Stephen Strasburg made his much-awaited MLB debut (STRASMAS) after recovering from Tommy John surgery (UCL reconstruction). He went for 14 strikeouts in seven innings. Nationals beat the Pirates 5-2. Attendance 40,315. It was a super-charged crowd that celebrated each strikeout amid a surge of hope for the NATS' future. Incredible experience.

How about 2015? The largest attendance was opening day, April 6, 2015, vs the Mets with Max Scherzer making his debut with the NATS. NATS lost 3-1.

is for...

BRYCE! Bryce Harper's Amazing 2015 Season:

A little Bio on Bryce (in case you missed it):

Bryce Aron Max Harper was born October 16, 1992, and after his sophomore year at Las Vegas High School he obtained his GED (graduated from HS to make himself eligible for the 2010 MLB Draft.) He played for the College of Southern Nevada Coyotes after high school.

Bryce honed his baseball skills in the back yard hitting bottle caps and red beans. According to a May 30, 2010 article (post gazette.com), his favorite movie was *The Sandlot.* At age 16, he was featured on the cover of *Sports Illustrated* magazine (June 8, 2010) with the headline, "Baseball's Chosen One."

Drafted #1 overall by the Nationals in 2010, he made his MLB debut on April 28, 2012. In 2012, he was selected for the All-Star Game, becoming the youngest position player ever elected. He was also voted the NL Rookie of the Year in 2012.

2015 Highlights:

NL MVP for 2015! The youngest to ever win the MVP award unanimously, receiving 30 first place votes! He is the third youngest in NL history to win, and the first ever for the Nats franchise (including the Expos). Previous D.C. winners of the MVP are Walter Johnson (1913, 1924) and Roger Peckinpaugh (1925).

Awarded the Esurance BEST MAJOR LEAGUER AWARD for 2015 (their top award), as well as BEST EVERYDAY PLAYER.

Awarded his first Silver Slugger Award in the outfield in 2015.

Also:

First player in modern MLB history to draw at least 4 walks, and score 4 runs and drive in 1 run without a hit or an at bat (September 3, 2015 vs the Braves). He saw 20 pitches from 3 pitchers in his 4 at bats, and the bat stayed put on his shoulder for all 20.

Awarded the Player of the Month in May 2015 for the first time in his career. He hit 3 home runs in his first 3 at bats (the record is 4) on May 6, 2015 at Nationals Park, all off of Marlins starter Tom Koehler. On May 9, Bryce Harper became the youngest player in MLB history to hit 5 home runs in a 2 game span.

One of 11 players to finish with a .330/.460/.640 slash line (OBP/SLG/OPS) and at least 40 home runs, joining the likes of Mickey Mantle (Yankees), Ted Williams (Red Sox), and Barry Bonds (Giants).

Awarded the 2015 NL Hank Aaron Award for offensive player of the year; Josh Donaldson (3B) of the Blue Jays won the AL award.

Awarded the 2015 Players Choice Award for National League (NL) Outstanding Player of the Year, an award voted on exclusively by MLB players.

Here are his 2015 Offensive Numbers:

#1 MLB—OPS (on base plus slugging %): 1.109

100 points ahead of Joey Votto (Reds)! The only other players to have such a lead at #1 have been Albert Pujols and Barry Bonds. Harper is #75 on the all-time list just ahead of Willie McCovey (1969 Giants) and Lou Gehrig (1931 Yankees), both with 1.108 OPS.

#1 MLB—SLG (slugging %): .649

#91 on the all-time list, Harper is just ahead of Lou Gehrig (1928 Yankees) and Ted Williams (1942 Red Sox), both with .648.

#1 MLB—OBP (on base %): .460

Harper is #84 on the all-time yearly list, tied with Eddie Collins (1915 White Sox), Shoeless Joe Jackson (1913 White Sox), Eddie Stanky (1950 Giants) and Paul O'Neill (1994 Yankees).

#1 MLB—WAR (wins above replacements) overall: 9.9 (tied with Zach Greinke RHP (Dodgers)

Other players with 9.9 WAR years: Roger Hornsby (1917-21 yrs old/ Cardinals), Ted Williams (1947-28 yrs old/Red Sox), Tris Speaker (1914-26 yrs old/Red Sox) and Sandy Koufax LHP (1963-27 yrs old/Dodgers).

#1 MLB—oWAR (offensive wins above replacements): 8.9 (tied with Mike Trout)

The only other players in history to achieve such a high oWAR in their age 22 seasons were Ty Cobb (9.5 in 1909) and Ted Williams (10.9 in 1941). Other players with 8.8 oWAR years: Willie Mays (1958-27 yrs old), Stan Musial (1946-25 yrs old) and Alex Rodriguez (2000-24 yrs old).

#1 MLB—RC (runs created): 161

At 161 RC, Harper is tied at #82 on the all-time list with Lou Gehrig (1932 Yankees), Jeff Bagwell (1999 Astros), Edgar Martinez (1995 Mariners), and John Olerud (1993 Blue Jays)

#1 MLB—WPA/LI (win probability divided by leverage index): 9.29

Almost 2 points ahead of Joey Votto (Reds) with 7.39, Harper is located at #4 on the all-time list! Barry Bonds holds the top three positions (2001, 2002, 2004 Giants), then Harper, and then Mark McGwire (1998 Cardinals).

#1 MLB—RE24 (run expectancy based on 24 base-out states): 79.31

Harper is #19 on the all-time list, just ahead of George Brett (1980 Royals), and Alex Rodriquez (2007 Yankees). Barry Bonds holds the top four positions on the list (2004, 2002, 2001, 1996).

2015 Rank	Category	Statistic
#1 NL	Runs	118
#1 NL (tied)	Home Runs	42
#2 MLB/NL	Walks	128
#1 MLB	RC27 (runs created per 27 outs)	10.61
#1 MLB	ISO (isolated power)	.319
#1 MLB	SECA (secondary average)	.560
#1 MLB	wRAA (weighted runs above average)	77.3
#1 MLB	wOBA (weighted on base average)	.461
#1 MLB	wRC+ (weighted runs created plus)	197
Career High	Games Played	153

(see fangraphs.com for explanations of the above stat categories)

BROADCASTERS—RADIO:

Charlie Slowes, Radio Play-by-Play: With the Nats since February 2005, his trademark "Bang! Zoom! Go the Fireworks" and "a curly 'W' is in the books" quickly became a permanent part of the Nats game experience. A graduate of Fordham University, Slowes began his broadcasting career with KMOX radio in St. Louis, where he worked with Bob Costas and the late HOF broadcaster, Jack Buck.

Dave Jaegler, Radio Play-by-Play: Jaegler joined the Nats from the Triple A Pawtucket Red Sox in 2006 and spent six years in Charlotte as the voice of UNC Charlotte basketball. He graduated from the S.I. Newhouse School of Public Communications at Syracuse University with a degree in broadcast journalism.

Fun Fact: The first Radio broadcast and Color Commentator: The first baseball game broadcast on radio was on August 5, 1921 by KDKA of Pittsburgh, the Pirates versus the Philadelphia Phillies (Pirates won 8-5). In game 3 of the 1923 World Series, Grantland Rice turned over the microphone to Graham McNamee (both were doing play by play), who became the first ever color commentator.

BROADCASTERS—TELEVISION:

Bob Carpenter, T.V. Play-by-Play: Carpenter came to the Nats in 2006, after ten years on T.V. and radio with the St. Louis Cardinals and sixteen seasons of MLB on ESPN. A St. Louis native, Carpenter won two St. Louis/Mid America Emmys. He has called 5 no-hitters, and publishes his own scorebook, *Bob Carpenter's Scorebook.*

F.P. (Frank-Paul) Santangelo, T.V. Color Analyst: Joining MASN and the Nats in 2011, he previously worked broadcasting San Francisco Giants games on radio. He made his Major League debut with the EXPOS in 1995, and was 4th in NL Rookie of the Year voting in 1996. He played under former Nationals manager Davey Johnson in 2000 (LA Dodgers).

Johnny Holliday, T.V. Host, Nats Xtra: In his sixth season with the MASN and the Nats, Holliday is also seeing his 34th season as the "Voice of the Maryland Terrapins," covering both football and basketball. Holliday started his career as a top-40 disc jockey, and worked with Murray the K at WINS in NYC. *The Washingtonian* honored Holliday as Washingtonian of the Year for his many civic activities, and he is also a member of the Radio Television Broadcasters Hall of Fame.

Ray Knight, T.V. Analyst, Nats Xtra: A two-time MLB all-star and MVP of the 1986 World Series with the New York Mets, Knight has been with the Nats since 2009. He played professional baseball for seventeen years as an infielder, thirteen of which were spent with the Reds, Astros, and Mets. As a Red, he replaced Pete Rose at 3rd base, and as a Met, he hit the winning run of game six in the 1986 World Series. He retired from MLB in 1989, and became an ESPN broadcaster in 1993.

Bryon Kerr and Phil Wood, Radio Hosts, Nats Talk Live: Into his seventh season with the Nats, Kerr was the voice of the Washington Mystics from 2000-06, and also covers the George Washington

University men's basketball team. Wood has spent his career in the D.C. Baltimore area (graduated from Thomas Jefferson HS in Fairfax County, VA), and published a book in 2005, *Nationals on Parade*.

Fun Fact: The FIRST T.V. Broadcast: The first televised MLB game took place on August 26, 1939, broadcast on station W2XBS (NYC), the station that was to become WNBC TV. HOF announcer Red Barber called the game between the Cincinnati Reds and the Brooklyn Dodgers at Ebbets Field in Brooklyn, NY. Barber was famous for a number of phrases, including "can of corn," describing an easily caught fly ball.

BATTERS—First Ever at RFK

First batter: Brad Wilkerson CF (Opening day April 4, 2005)

First base hit: Brad Wilkerson CF (in first at bat on April 4, 2005)

First grand slam: Brad Wilkerson CF (August 4, 2005)

First "hit for the cycle": Brad Wilkerson CF (second game of first season, 2005)

Note: Wilkerson hit a "natural cycle" on June 24, 2003 for the Montreal Expos

BATTERS—First Ever at Nationals PARK

First hit in Nationals Park: Cristian Guzman SS (March 30, 2008)

First walk off home run at Nationals Park: Ryan Zimmerman 3B on opening day of the first year (March 31, 2008)

First "hit for the cycle" at Nationals Park: Cristian Guzman SS (August 20, 2008)

First grand slam: Felipe Lopez 2B—1 (April 24, 2008)

BATTING Average—
Leaders Each Season *(#1-2-3 highlighted):*

Year	Batting Avg.	Leader
2005	.289	Nick Johnson 1B
2006	.290	Nick Johnson 1B
2007	.320	Dmitri Young 1B (#2)
2008	.316	Cristian Guzman SS
2009	.295	Nick Johnson 1B
2010	.307	Ryan Zimmerman
2011	.303	Michael Morse 1B
2012	.300	Jayson Werth RF
2013	.318	Jayson Werth RF (#3)
2014	.302	Denard Span CF
2015	.330	Bryce Harper (#1)(#2 in NL & #3 in MLB)

Batting Average—Fun Fact: The top MLB single season batting average record (since 1900) is held by Nap Lajoie 2B with .426 (1901—Philadelphia Athletics). Since 1920, Roger Hornsby 2B (Cardinals) has the highest with .424 in 1924, and since 1940, Ted Williams (.406 in 1941—last average over .400).

BB (BASES ON BALLS)—Leaders
Each Season *(#1-2-3 highlighted):*

Year	Base on Balls	Leader
2005	84	Brad Wilkerson CF
2006	110	Nick Johnson 1B (#3)
2007	71	Austin Kearns RF
2008	50	Elijah Dukes RF
2009	116	Adam Dunn 1B (#2)
2010	77	Adam Dunn 1B
2011	74	Jayson Werth RF
2012	67	Adam LaRoche 1B
2013	72	Adam LaRoche 1B
2014	83	Jayson Werth RF
2015	124	Bryce Harper OF (#1) (#2 MLB & #2 NL)

Fun Fact: The top MLB single season Bases on Balls record is held by Barry Bonds LF (Giants) with 232 in 2004. Bonds holds the #2 and #3 records as well with 198 in 2002, and 177 in 2001. Babe Ruth (OF) (Yankees) comes in #4 with 170 in 1923.

C is for...

CATCHERS STATS:

Fun Fact: The catcher's armor (shin guards, mask, glove and chest protector) was jokingly given the name of "tools of ignorance" by Herold "Muddy" Ruel, a catcher for the Washington Senators/Nationals in the 1920s for the likes of Walter Johnson. Adoption of protective gear came slowly, and not without ridicule by spectators. HOF catcher Roger Bresnahan (Giants) added the final piece—shin guards—in 1907 to a somewhat negative crowd at the Polo Grounds.

CATCHERS: Most Games Caught—Leaders Each Season (% of games) (innings, starts) (top season highlighted) *(baseball reference.com and fangraphs.com)*

2005: 113 games—*Brian Schneider* (69.75%) (926.2 innings, started 105 games)

2006: 123 games—*Brian Schneider* (75.92%) (990.1 innings, started 111 games)

2007: 122 games— *Brian Schneider* (75.30%) (1051.1 innings, started 120 games)

2008: 82 games— *Jesus Flores* (50.61%) (673.0 innings, started 78 games)

2009: 79 games— *Josh Bard* (48.76%) (630.2 innings, started 71 games)

2010: 102 games— *Ivan Rodriguez* (62.96%) (884.0 innings, started 102 games)

2011: 108 games— *Wilson Ramos* (66.66%) (951.2 innings, started 106 games)

2012: 80 games—*Jesus Flores* (49.38%) (687.2 innings, started 75 games)

2013: 79 games— *Kurt Suzuki* (48.14%)(659.0 innings, started 73 games)

2014: 87 games—*Wilson Ramos* (53.70%) (775.0 innings, started 87 games)

2015: 125 games—*Wilson Ramos* (77.16%) (1078.1 innings, started 123 games)

Fun Fact: The record holder for most games caught in a season is Randy Hundley (Cubs) with 160 in 1968, an amazing 98.6% of the total games.

CATCHERS—Most Total Games with the Nats *(2005 through 2014):*

#1—*Wilson Ramos* 436 (3,818.2 innings)

#2—*Brian Schneider* 358 (2,968.1 innings)

#3—*Jesus Flores* 263 (2,154.2 innings)

Fun Fact: The record holder for most games caught in a career is

Carlton Fisk with 2,226, and highest career percentage of games caught is Jason Kendall with 80.65%.

CATCHERS: Offensive Numbers

(minimum 100 plate appearances):

CATCHERS: OPS Catchers (On Base Plus Slugging Percentage)— Leader Each Season *(#1-2-3 highlighted):*

Year	OPS	Player
2005	.739	Brian Schneider
2006	.667	Robert Fick
2007	.661	Brian Schneider
2008	.698	Jesus Flores
2009	.877	Jesus Flores (#1)
2010	.640	Ivan Rodriguez
2011	.779	Wilson Ramos (#2)
2012	.725	Kurt Suzuki
2013	.777	Wilson Ramos (#3)
2014	.698	Wilson Ramos
2015	.616	Wilson Ramos

Fun Fact: Mike Piazza (Dodgers) holds the single season OPS record for catchers with 1.070 in 1997.

CATCHERS: Batting Average (BA)— Leader Each Season (with HR and RBI noted)

(#1-2-3 highlighted):

Year	OPS	Player
2005	.268	Brian Schneider (#3) (10 HR, 44 RBI)
2006	.256	Brian Schneider (4 HR, 55 RBI)
2007	.235	Brian Schneider (6 HR, 54 RBI)
2008	.261	Wil Nieves (1 HR, 20 RBI)
2009	.301	Jesus Flores (#1) (4 HR, 15 RBI)
2010	.266	Ivan Rodriguez (4 HR, 49 RBI)
2011	.267	Wilson Ramos (15 HR, 52 RBI)
2012	.267	Kurt Suzuki (5 HR, 25 RBI)
2013	.272	Wilson Ramos (#2) (16 HR, 59 RBI)
2014	.267	Wilson Ramos (11 HR, 47 RBI)
2015	.229	Wilson Ramos

Fun Fact: Joe Mauer (Twins) holds the record for highest single season catcher batting average with .365 in 2009. That year, he was the first catcher to lead the AL in OBP, Slugging %, and batting average in a single year since George Brett in 1980.

COACHES 2015— and Assorted Staff

Mike Maddux—Pitching Coach, replacing Steve McCatty for 2016 season

- Pitching coach for the Brewers (2003-09) and the Rangers (2009-15). Made his coaching debut with the Round Rock Express (AA Astros).

- Pitched fifteen years from 1986-2000, starting out with the Phillies. Compiled a record of 39 wins, 564 strikeouts, and a 4.05 ERA.

- Older brother of pitcher Greg Maddux.

- Previous pitching coaches: Steve McCatty (2009-15), Randy St. Claire (2005-09)

Rick Schu — Hitting Coach, re-hired for 2016

- With the Nats since 2009, replaced Rick Eckstein on July 23, 2013, let go at the end of 2015.

- Seventeen seasons as a hitting coach and a nine year big league career.

- Played primarily 3rd base for the Philadelphia Phillies

- Two seasons in Japan for the Nippon Ham Fighters

- 2007-09 hitting coach for the Arizona Diamondbacks

- Father, Ken, pitched for the Chicago White Sox system in 1955

- Previous hitting coaches: Rick Eckstein (2009-13), Lenny Harris (2007-08), Mitchell Page (2006), Tommy McCraw (2005)

Bob Henley, Third Base Coach (Re-hired for 2016)

- Minor league manager in the EXPOS system when they relocated to D.C. in 2005

- Promoted to third base coach on November 19, 2013; fired with all the coaches in 2015 at the end of the season

- One of three former big league catchers on the Nats coaching staff (Randy Knorr, Matt LeCroy)

- Made his major league debut with the Montreal EXPOS on September 26, 1998.

- Previous third base coaches: Trent Jewett (2013), Bo Porter (2011-12), Pat Listach (2009-10), Tim Tolman (2007-08), Tony Beasley (2006), Dave Huppert (2005)

Jacques Jones—Assistant Hitting Coach, a new position for the Nats

- Outfielder drafted by the Twins, made his MLB debut in June 1999.

- Played for the Twins (1999-2005), Cubs (2006-07), Tigers (2007), and Marlins (2008).

- .277 Career batting average, 165 home runs and 630 RBI.

Davey Lopes—First Base Coach

- Dodgers first base coach 2010-15, previously with the Nats 2005-06

- Teammate with Nats manager Dusty Baker 1976-81 (Dodgers); godfather to Baker's daughter, Natosha.

- MLB player (2B) from 1972-87, stealing a then Major League record 38 consecutive bases without getting caught stealing in 1975

- Previous first base coaches: Tony Tarasco (2013-15), Trent Jewett (2011-12), Dan Radison (2010), Marquis Grissom (2009), Jerry Morales (2007-08), Davey Lopes (2005-06), Don Buford (2005)

Chris Speier—Bench Coach

- Nineteen seasons as SS, mainly with the Giants, Expos, and Cubs; 3 time All-Star.

- Winner of the 1987 Willie Mac Award for his spirit and leadership with the Giants.

- Third base coach with the Cubs 2005-06, and bench coach with the Reds 2007-12.

- Previous bench coaches: Randy Knorr (2012-15), Pat Corrales (2011), John McClaren (2010-11), Pat Corrales (2009), Jim Riggleman (2009), Pat Corrales (2007-2008), Eddie Rodriguez (2005-06)

Dan Firova — Bullpen Coach

- Twenty seasons as a manager and coach, mostly in the Mexican League — won three league championships

- Former catcher (like Randy Knorr, Matt LeCroy, and Bob Henley), drafted by the Mariners in 1980, spent thirteen years in the minor leagues in the U.S. and Mexico, played in 17 MLB games with the Mariners and Indians.

- Previous bullpen coaches: Matthew LeCroy (2014-15), Jim Lett (2010-13), Randy Knorr (2009), Rick Aponte (2007-08), Randy Knorr (2006), John Wetteland (2006), Bob Natal (2005)

Spin Williams — Senior Baseball Advisor/Pitching Consultant

- Prior to joining the Nats in 2006, spent twenty-seven years with the Pittsburgh Pirates:

- Minor league pitcher (1979-81)

- Pitching instructor and manager (1981-93)

- Pirates major league coaching staff for twelve consecutive seasons – bullpen coach (1994-2000) and pitching coach (2001-2005).

Rick Ankiel — Life Skills Coordinator

- Pitcher with the Cardinals from 1999-2004, switched to the outfield playing for the Royals and Braves in 2010, Nationals 2011-12, and the Astros and Mets in 2013.

- He was the first player since BABE RUTH to have won at least 10 games as a pitcher and also hit at least 50 home runs.

2015 Coaches—Who Moved to other Positions in the Nats Organization in October 2015

Randy Knorr, Bench Coach: named senior assistant to the GM

Matthew LeCroy, Bullpen Coach: named manager of Double A Harrisburg

CHARITIES—Nats Supporting the Community

Dream Foundation

The Nationals Dream Foundation raises money to improve the lives of children and teens throughout the Nats area, providing support through the following programs:

- The Washington Nationals Youth Baseball Academy

- The Washington Nationals Diabetes Care Complex at Children's National Medical Center

- The Neighborhood Initiative

- The Washington Nationals Miracle Field

***For more information on programs or how to donate, see the Washington Nationals website.

ziMS Foundation

Founded by Nat Ryan Zimmerman, the foundation is dedicated to the treatment and ultimate cure of Multiple Sclerosis. For more info, visit www.zimsfoundation.org.

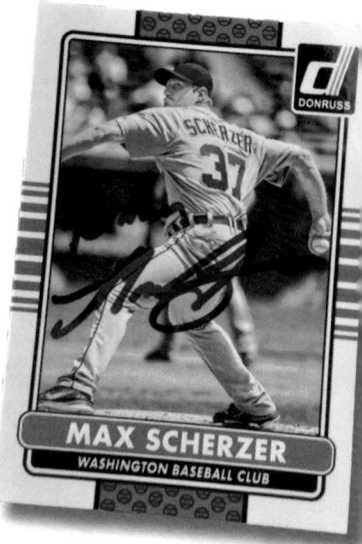

Baseball Cards for a Cause

Max Scherzer partnered with the Dream Foundation to raise money in exchange for a signed baseball card. For more info, visit the Washington Nationals website.

DOUBLES—Leaders Each Season

(#1-2-3 highlighted)

Year	Doubles	Player
2005	42	Brad Wilkerson CF
2006	47, 46	Ryan Zimmerman 3B (#1, 47), Nick Johnson 1B (#2, 46)
2007	43	Ryan Zimmerman 3B and Ryan Church LF (tied #3)
2008	35	Cristian Guzman SS
2009	37	Ryan Zimmerman 3B
2010	36	Adam Dunn 1B
2011	36	Michael Morse 1B
2012	37	Danny Espinosa 2B
2013	38	Ian Desmond SS
2014	39	Anthony Rendon 3B
2015	38	Bryce Harper OF

Fun Fact: The all-time MLB single season leader is Earl Webb RF (Red Sox) with 67 in 1931.

DRAFT PICKS—Nats Top Draft Picks (by year) (#1 picks highlighted):

2005: #4 (1st round)—*Ryan Zimmerman (3B)*, University of Virginia

2006: #15 (1st round)—*Christopher Marrero (OF)*, Monsignor Edward Pace HS

2007: #6 (1st round)—*Ross Detwiler (LHP)*, Missouri State University

2008: #9 (1st round)—*Aaron Crow (LHP)*, University of Missouri

2009: #1 (1st round)—*Stephen Strasburg (RHP)*, San Diego State

2010: #1 (1st round)—*Bryce Harper (C)*, College of Southern Nevada

2011: #6 (1st round)—*Anthony Rendon (3B)*, Rice University

2012: #16 (1st round)—*Lucas Giolito (RHP)*, Harvard Westlake HS

2013: #68 (2nd round)—*Jake Johansen (RHP)*, Dallas Baptist University

2014: #18 (1st round)—*Erick Fedde (RHP)*, University of Nevada Las Vegas

2015: #58 (2nd round)—*Andrew Stevenson (OF)*, Louisiana State University

D is for D.C. BASEBALL: Some History

Washington Senators

In the modern period since 1901, there were two Washington Senators teams: the 1901-60 Senators—who moved to become the Minnesota Twins--and the 1961-71 Senators, formed as an expansion team after the Senators' move in 1960, who relocated to become the Texas Rangers.

Highlights:

- Founded in 1901 as one of the American League's eight charter franchises

- 1905, after a 113 loss season in 1904, name was changed to "Nationals" (nicknamed the Nats); Senators name was still used but not officially again until 1956

- Given the somewhat rocky start, the Senators suffered jokes like "Washington: First in war, first in peace, and last in the American League" (Charley Dryden of the San Francisco Chronicle)

- Things turned around from 1911 to 1933 with players such as:

  Walter Johnson "The Big Train" RHP—HOF 1936
  Goose Goslin IF —HOF 1968
  Sam Rice OF—HOF 1963
  Joe Cronin SS—HOF 1956
  Bucky Harris 2B—HOF 1975
  Heinie Manush LF—HOF 1964

- 1924 World Champions—led by player manager Bucky Harris—victorious over John McGraw's New York Giants

- 1925 American League Pennant—lost to Pittsburgh

- 1960 Washington Senators moved to Minnesota to become the Twins, and they were replaced an expansion team in 1961

- Frank Howard ("Hondo") was a favorite for many, winning two home run titles

- HOF hitter Ted Williams was named manager in 1967

- With mixed or less success, this Senators team was moved to Texas (Rangers) for the 1972 season

Homestead Grays—Negro Leagues

Formed 1912 by Cumberland Posey (HOF 2006) in Homestead, Pennsylvania, the Grays moved to Pittsburgh but began playing half of their home games in D.C. in 1940 at Griffith Stadium (home of the Washington Senators).

When playing at Griffith, they were known as the Washington Homestead Grays or Washington Grays.

The Grays were a storied franchise featuring HOF players Josh Gibson (C), Cool Papa Bell (P), Ray Brown (P), Buck Leonard (1B), Jud Wilson (3B), and Smokey Joe Williams (3B)

ERA—STARTING PITCHERS
Leaders Each Season (#1-2-3 highlighted):

2005:	3.13	John Patterson
2006:	5.57	Ramon Ortiz
2007:	4.63	Matt Chico
2008:	3.91	John Lannan
2009:	3.88	John Lannan
2010:	3.66	Livan Hernandez
2011:	3.18	Jordan Zimmermann
2012:	2.89	Gio Gonzalez
2013:	3.00	Stephen Strasburg
2014:	2.41	Doug Fister 2.41 (#1),
	2.62	Jordan Zimmermann (#2)
2015:	2.79	Max Scherzer #3

Fun Fact: The Single Season ERA record was set by Dutch Leonard (Red Sox) with 0.961 in 1914 at age 22; Mordecai "Three Finger" Brown (Cubs) had 1.04 in 1906. Since 1920, the leader is Bob Gibson (Cardinals) with 1.12 in 1968 (known as the "Year of the Pitcher," after which the strike zone was adjusted back to pre-1963 and the pitching mound lowered from 15 to 10 inches).

ERA Minus (ERA-)—Starting Pitchers Leaders Each Season *(#1-2-3 highlighted):*

(FANGRAPHS.COM)

Note: ERA- (minus) reflects how much better the pitcher is than league average. A score of 100 would be an average level performance, below 100 is better. For example, if the score is 86, that means the pitcher is 14% better than league average that season. (For more info, go to fangraphs.com.)

Year	ERA-	Player
2005	77	John Patterson
2006	102	John Patterson
2007	80	Shawn Hill
2008	91	John Lannan
2009	93	John Lannan
2010	91	Livan Hernandez
2011	83	Jordan Zimmermann
2012	73	Gio Gonzalez
2013	80	Stephen Strasburg
2014	66, 72	Doug Fister (#1, 66) Jordan Zimmermann (#3, 72)
2015	71	Max Scherzer (#2)

Fun Fact: Best Single Season ERA- (since 1900) belongs to Pedro Martinez (Red Sox) who had 35 in 2000 (his ERA that year was 1.74). In 1968, Bob Gibson's (Cardinals) ERA- was 38; his ERA was 1.12. Gibson is 4th on the list behind Martinez, Dutch Leonard (Red Sox) with 36 in 1914, and Greg Maddux (Braves) with 37 in 1994.

ERA—RELIEVERS/CLOSERS
Leaders Each Season (#1-2-3 highlighted)

2005:	1.82	Chad Cordero (#2)
2006:	3.19	Chad Cordero
2007:	3.36	Chad Cordero
2008:	2.16	Steven Shell
2009:	2.69	Tyler Clippard
2010:	2.02	Joel Peralta
2011:	1.83	Tyler Clippard (#3)
2012:	2.34	Craig Stammen
2013:	1.51	Tanner Roark
2014:	1.12	Drew Storen (#1)
2015:	2.18	Matt Thornton

ERA Minus (ERA-)—RELIEVERS/CLOSERS
Leaders Each Season (#1-2-3 highlighted)

Year	ERA-	Player
2005	45	Chad Cordero (#2)
2006	74	Chad Cordero
2007	79	Chad Cordero
2008	50	Steven Shell
2009	64	Tyler Clippard
2010	50	Joel Peralta
2011	48	Tyler Clippard (#3)
2012	59	Craig Stammen
2013	64	Tyler Clippard
2014	30	Drew Storen (#1)
2015	55	Matt Thornton

ERRORS—
Leaders Each Season *(#1-2-3 highlighted):*

2005:	15	Cristian Guzman SS
2006:	15	Nick Johnson 1B and Ryan Zimmerman 3B
2007:	23	Ryan Zimmerman 3B
2008:	17	Cristian Guzman SS
2009:	20	Cristian Guzman SS
2010:	34	Ian Desmond SS (#1) (#1 in MLB)
2011:	23	Ian Desmond SS
2012:	19	Ryan Zimmerman 3B
2013:	21	Ryan Zimmerman 3B
2014:	24	Ian Desmond SS (#3)
2015:	27	Ian Desmond SS (#2) (#1 in NL, #2 in MLB)

Fun Fact: Since 1910, the single season leader in errors is Buck Weaver SS/3B (White Sox) who had 71 errors in 1912. Since 2000, Jose Valentin IF (White Sox) is the leader with 36 in 2000.

E is also for EQUIPMENT:

NATS GLOVES AND BATS

What brand of bats and gloves do the current Nationals favor? Keeping in mind that some players change around sometimes (especially Bryce Harper), the players have been noted in photographs and at games with the following:

Pitchers Gloves:

- Max Scherzer — Rawlings
- Stephen Strasburg — Nike
- Gio Gonzalez — Wilson
- Drew Storen — Mizuno
- Craig Stammen — TPX
- Jordan Zimmermann — Mizuno

Fielder Gloves:

- Jayson Werth — Rawlings
- Ian Desmond — Marucci
- Wilson Ramos — Wilson
- Ryan Zimmerman — Rawlings
- Bryce Harper — Rawlings
- Denard Span — Rawling

Fun Fact: According to a USA Today article (Scott Boeck, March 18, 2013), Bryce Harper's dad, Ron, had his own method for breaking in his son's glove: he stuffed 3 balls into the glove, tied it shut and dropped it in a bucket of water for a day. After removal from the water, Ron smashed it with a sledgehammer, and then repeated everything a second time, and then letting it dry out for a day before Bryce used it. Bryce said it shortens the time he needs to break it in, and that it comes out ready to go. He also uses saddle oil on his glove.

Bats:

- Anthony Rendon—Marucci

- Bryce Harper—Chandler

- Wilson Ramos—Chandler

- Danny Espinosa—Tucci

- Ian Desmond—Mizuno

- Jose Lobaton—Max Bat

- Jayson Werth—Max Bat

- Ryan Zimmerman—Louisville Slugger

Fun Fact: According to a Washington Post article (Isabelle Khurshudyan, July 25, 2014), many Nats players like maple bats because they are harder; they break less often than ash, but they break more violently when they do. Because of this, MLB imposed a regulation for the slope of grain in maple bats. Yellow birch is becoming more popular because it is also hard. Bryce Harper and Ian Desmond keep their bats in a temperature controlled humidor, a practice popularized by Ichiro Suzuki . Barry Bonds used a maple bat to break the single season home run record in 2001. In 2013, about 70 percent of MLB players used maple bats, 25 percent ash and 5 percent yellow birch.

MORE FUN FACTS: INTERESTING INFO ABOUT BASEBALLS—THINGS YOU SHOULD KNOW:

- The official MLB ball is made by Rawlings (since 1977) in Costa Rica, in the town of Turrialba; previously they were made in Haiti. The balls are handmade, including the 108 red stitches. The factory produces as many as 2.4 million balls per year.

- In the early 1900s, the game ball was used until it was no longer playable (mangled, etc.). A baseball was very expensive then (reportedly equal to about $40 today) and fans returned foul balls and the rare home run.

- Modern day teams use 8 to 10 dozen baseballs per game; a ball is lucky to make it through 8 pitches!

- Magic Mud: Since the 1950s, All Major and Minor League game baseballs are rubbed with Lena Blackburne rubbing mud before a game to give them a bit of a rougher surface. The mud comes from a secret location on the New Jersey side of the Delaware River.

- "The Humidor": In 2002, the Colorado Rockies began storing their baseballs in an atmosphere controlled environment known locally as "the humidor" in order to counteract the impact of Denver's mile high dry climate.

- Who Knew? Baseballs have a "shelf life," meaning that teams may not use "last year" baseballs in games, though they can be used for batting practice.

- Printed Signatures on baseballs: The NL and AL used to have their own balls, signed by the league presidents. Reportedly the first NL president to sign was Harry Pulliam in 1908, AL was Ban Johnson in 1901. In 2000, baseballs became "MLB" and are signed by the commissioner. Rob Manfred is the first commission to BEGIN his term with his signature on every baseball.

F is for Nats **FIRSTS**— First Ever at RFK:

First Ever Nats Batter: Brad Wilkerson CF—got a hit in this first at bat on April 04, 2005. He was the last ever Montreal Expos batter because he wore the Expos uniform during a MLB Japan All-Star Series after the end of the 2004 regular season; as such his is sometimes referred to as "The Last Expo." (WIK)

First Ceremonial Pitches at both RFK and the new Nationals Park: President George W. Bush on April 14, 2005 and March 30, 2008

First Nats Manager: Frank Robinson

First Nats Starter: Livan Hernandez on April 04, 2005 (loss to the Phillies). Hernandez was also the first starter at home (RFK) on April 14, 2005 when he threw eight shutout innings for the win against the Diamondbacks.

First Nats Save: Chad Cordero on April 12, 2005

First Nats Grand Slam: Brad Wilkerson CF on August 04, 2005

First "Hit for the Cycle": Brad Wilkerson CF, in the second game of the 2005 season. Wilkerson previously hit for a "natural cycle" on June 24, 2003 as a Montreal Expo. The only other "cycle" to date by the Nats was by Cristian Guzman at Nationals Park on August 20, 2008

First Ever Home Run: Termel Sledge LF on April 4, 2005

First Ever Bases Empty Inside the Park Home Run: Austin Kearns RF on May 12, 2007

First STATS MLB Leader: Chad Cordero #1 in saves with 47 in 2005

First All-Stars: Livan Hernandez P and Chad Cordero P (2005)

First (and only) 20 Game Winner: Gio Gonzalez–21 wins in 2012

First NO-HITTER: Jordan Zimmermann on September 28, 2014, the last game of the regular season

First and only IMMACULATE INNING (struck out 3 batters on nine consecutive pitches in a half inning): Jordan Zimmermann on May 6, 2011 vs the Florida Marlins

First Nats Manager of the Year: Davey Johnson 2012. Matt Williams was second in 2014.

First Nats Rookie of the Year: Bryce Harper 2012

MORE FIRSTS—
First Ever at Nationals PARK:

First Home Run (and walk off) in Nationals Park: Ryan Zimmerman's (3B) two out walk off home run in the bottom of the 9th inning on opening day, March 30, 2008. Chipper Jones of the Atlanta Braves hit the first home run in the park earlier in the game.

First Pitcher/Starter in Nationals Park: Odalis Perez. Jon Rauch got the win.

First Hit in Nationals Park: Cristian Guzman SS March 30, 2008. Guzman also scored the first run

First RBI in Nationals Park: Nick Johnson 1B March 30, 2008

First ERROR in Nationals Park: Christian Guzman SS on opening day, March 30, 2008

First Grand Slam in Nationals Park: Felipe Lopez 2B on April 24, 2008

FIELDING STATS—Nats who were MLB Single Season Leaders *(#1 in MLB):*

#1 in MLB for Putouts as 3B:
Vinny Castilla 2005
Ryan Zimmerman 2007
Ryan Zimmerman 2009
Anthony Rendon 2014

#1 in MLB for Putouts as OF:
Alfonso Soriano as LF 2006
Denard Span as CF 2014

#1 in MLB for Fielding % as CF:
Denard Span 2013

#1 in MLB for Double Plays:

Alfonso Soriano as OF/LF 2006
Ryan Zimmerman as 3B 2007
Bryce Harper as OF/LF 2013
Denard Span as CF/OF 2014

#1 in MLB for Assists:

Ryan Zimmerman as 3B 2007 and 2009
Alfonso Soriano as LF 2006
Bryce Harper as LF 2014

#1 in MLB for Defensive Games:

Ian Desmond as SS 2014
Ian Desmond as SS 2015

#1 in MLB for fielding % as Pitcher

Livan Hernandez 2010
Stephen Strasburg and Dan Haren (tied) 2013

#1 in Total Zone Runs as Catcher

Wilson Ramos 2015

FIP: Field Independent Pitching—
STARTING PITCHERS—Leaders Each Season

Year	FIP	Player
2005	3.33	Esteban Loiza
2006	5.46	Ramon Ortiz
2007	5.56	Matt Chico
2008	4.79	John Lannan
2009	4.70	John Lannan
2010	3.95	Livan Hernandez
2011	3.16	Jordan Zimmermann
2012	2.82	Gio Gonzalez (#3)
2013	3.21	Stephen Strasburg
2014	2.68	Jordan Zimmermann (#1)
2015	2.77	Max Scherzer (#2)

Fun Fact: The best single season FIP record belongs to Christy Mathewson (Giants) with 1.287 in 1908; Walter Johnson (Senators) is second with 1.387 (1910) and Pedro Martinez (Red Sox) third with 1.395 (1999)

FLY OUTS (AO)—HITTERS—Leaders Each Season (#1-2-3 Nat highlighted)

2005:	173	Brad Wilkerson CF
2006:	205	Alfonso Soriano LF (#1)
2007:	185	Ryan Zimmerman 3B (#2)
2008:	143	Cristian Guzman SS

2009:	180	Ryan Zimmerman 3B
2010:	144	Ryan Zimmerman 3B
2011:	143	Danny Espinosa 2B
2012:	165	Adam LaRoche 1B
2013:	146	Adam LaRoche 1B
2014:	184	Denard Span CF (#3)
2015:	111	Ian Desmond SS

Fun Fact: Nomar Garciaparra SS (Red Sox) with 254 in 2003 is tied with Jimmie Rollins SS (Phillies), who had 254 in 2007, for the single season record in Fly Outs.

is for...

GOLD GLOVE AWARD WINNERS—Two Times for Nats:

Ryan Zimmerman 3B—Gold Glove Award 2009
Adam La Roche 1B—Gold Glove Award 2012

MORE AWARDS: SILVER SLUGGER AWARD WINNERS—Nine Times for Nats:

Alfonso Soriano OF—Silver Slugger Award 2006
Ryan Zimmerman 3B—2 time Silver Slugger Award (2009, 2010)
Ian Desmond SS—3 time Silver Slugger Award (2012, 2013, 2014)
Stephen Strasburg RHP—Silver Slugger Award 2012
Anthony Rendon 3B—Silver Slugger Award 2014
Bryce Harper—Silver Slugger Award 2015

NATS GRAND SLAMS: Leaders—Who had the Most: Ryan ZIMMERMAN

Ryan Zimmerman 3B—5 (2 are walk off grand slams!)
Michael Morse 1B—4
Josh Willingham LF—3

Fun Fact: The single season record for grand slams is shared by Travis Hafner DH (Indians) with 6 in 2006, and Don Mattingly 1B (Yankees) with 6 in 1987.

COMPLETE LIST (NOTABLE GRAND SLAMS HIGHLIGHTED):

2005	Brad Wilkerson CF—1 (August 4, 2005)
2006	Ryan Church CF—1 (April 18, 2006)
	Alfonso Soriano LF—1 (June 4, 2006)
2007	Ryan Zimmerman 3B—2 (April 22 2007 and walk off grand slam May 12, 2007)
	Felipe Lopez SS—1 (May 22, 2007)
	Ryan Langerhans CF—1 (May 27, 2007)
	Dmitri Young 1B—1 (July 1, 2007)
	Justin Maxwell OF—1 (September 11, 2007)
2008	Felipe Lopez SS—1 (April 24, 2008)—First at Nationals Park
	Jesus Flores SS—1 (May 28, 2008)
	Ronnie Belliard IF—1 (July 2, 2008)
	Willie Harris LF—1 (August 22, 2008)
2009	Austin Kearns RF—2 (March 21, 2009 and April 18 2009)
	Adam Dunn 1B—2 (May 24, 2009 and July 25, 2009)
	Josh Willingham LF—2 (in one game! July 27, 2009)
	Ronnie Belliard 2B—1 (August 22, 2009)

	Elijah Dukes RF—1 (August 26, 2009)
	Justin Maxwell CF—1 (walk off, September 30, 2009— first MLB career hit!)
2010	Josh Willingham LF—1 (April 11, 2010)
	Danny Espinosa 2B—1 September 6, 2010)
	Justin Maxwell CF—1 (September 17, 2010)
2011	Michael Morse 1B —2 (May 27, 2011 and June 5, 2011)
	Jerry Hairston, Jr. 3B—1 (July 22, 2011)
	Rick Ankiel CF—1 (August 2, 2011)
	Ryan Zimmerman 3B—1 (August 19, 2011—walk off grand slam)
2012	Michael Morse 1B—2 (August 18, 2012 and September 29, 2012—first called a single!)
2013	Ryan Zimmerman 3B—1 (July 7, 2013)
	Ian Desmond SS—1 (June 19, 2013)
	Wilson Ramos C—1 (July 28, 2013)
2014	Jayson Werth RF—1 (April 9, 2014)
	Ian Desmond SS—1 (April 10, 2014)
2015	Michael Taylor OF—1 (May 13, 2015)
	Jayson Werth OF—1 (September 14, 2015)
	Wilson Ramos C—1 (September 7, 2015)
	Ryan Zimmerman 1B—1 (August 25, 2015)

Fun Facts: Don Mattingly 1B (Yankees) holds the record for single season grand slams with 6 in 1987; oddly, those were the only grand slams of his career. Fernando Tatis 3B (Cardinals) hit two grand slams in one inning off of Dodgers pitcher Chan Ho Park in the third inning on April 23, 1999. The single season National League leaders in grand slams are Ernie Banks SS (Cubs—1955) and Albert Pujols 1B (Cardinals—2009) who are tied with 5 each.

GROUNDED OUT (GO)—Hitters—
Leaders Each Season *(#1-2-3 highlighted):*

Year	GO	Player
2005	182	Cristian Guzman (#2)
2006	158	Ryan Zimmerman
2007	210	Felipe Lopez (#3)
2008	211	Cristian Guzman
2009	200	Cristian Guzman
2010	194	Nyger Morgan
2011	194	Ian Desmond
2012	187	Ryan Zimmerman
2013	236	Denard Span (#1)
2014	168	Anthony Rendon
2015	213	Yunel Escobar

Fun Fact: Juan Pierre CF (Marlins) holds the record for single season ground outs with 316 in 2003.

GROUNDED INTO DOUBLE PLAY (GIDP)—
Hitters—Leaders Each Season *(#1-2-3 highlighted):*

2005:	16	Vinny Castilla
2006:	16	Jose Vidro
2007:	26	Ryan Zimmerman (#1)
2008:	19	Lastings Milledge
2009:	22	Ryan Zimmerman
2010:	25	Ivan Rodriguez (#2)
2011:	19	Wilson Ramos
2012:	20	Ryan Zimmerman
2013:	16	Ian Desmond
2014:	17	Wilson Ramos
2015:	24	Yunel Escobar (#3)

Fun Fact: Since tracking started in 1933, Jim Rice LF (Red Sox) holds the record with 36 in 1984. Cal Ripken, Jr. SS (Orioles), grounded into the most double plays in MLB history with a total of 350 in his career.

GROUNDSKEEPER

John Turnour is the Director, Field Operations—or Head Groundskeeper—since February 2010. He has a degree in turf management from North Carolina State University, and previously worked as an Assistant Groundskeeper for the Orioles and Padres.

According to a Washington Post article by Steve Hendrix ("Washington Nationals' John Turnour Keeps the Field Perfectly Manicured" dated April 20, 2012):

- The field is 2.2 acres of Kentucky bluegrass

- Turnour considers the field a "10th player"

- He mows the grass himself

- The grass is kept at 1 and 1/16 inches during the spring

- He has no lawn at his Arlington apartment

Turnour has help! According to MLB.com, each club has 20 plus full time, part time, and seasonal grounds crew members. Their day begins with "scout turfing" (!), i.e. examining the turf for disease and stress. They monitor the irrigation system, maintain proper moisture levels, aerate weak areas, top dress, seed, drag, cover/uncover the field, and set up for batting practice and drills.

Fun Fact: The most famous groundskeeper would probably be Groundskeeper Willie of "The Simpsons," head groundskeeper at Springfield Elementary School.

is for...

HITTING: All-Time Nats LEADERS—Single Season

(MLB.COM)

Batting Average:	Bryce Harper OF— .330 (2015)
HR:	Alfonso Soriano LF—46 (2006)
RBI:	Ryan Zimmerman 3B—110 (2006)
Strikeouts:	Adam Dunn 1B—199 (2010)
OBP:	Bryce Harper OF—.460 (2015)
Slugging:	Bryce Harper OF—.649 (2015)
OPS:	Bryce Harper OF —1.109 (2015)
Hits:	Denard Span CF—184 (2014)
2B:	Ryan Zimmerman 3B—47 (2006)
3B:	Denard Span CF —11 (2013)
Runs:	Alfonso Soriano LF—119 (2006)
Extra Base Hits:	Alfonso Soriano LF—89 (2006)
Total Bases:	Alfonso Soriano—362 (2009)

Stolen Bases:	Alfonso Soriano LF—41 (2006)
Caught Stealing:	Nyger Morgan CF—17 (2010)
BB (Bases on Balls):	Bryce Harper—124 (2015)
IBB (Intentional Bases on Balls):	Adam Dunn—16 (2009), Alfonso Soriano—16 (2006)
At Bats:	Ryan Zimmerman 3B—653 (2007)
Games Played:	Ryan Zimmerman 3B—162 (2007)
HBP (Hit by Pitch):	Danny Espinosa 2B—19 (2012)
SF (Sacrifice Flies):	Ryan Zimmerman 1B—10 (2015)
SAC (Sacrifice Bunts):	Livan Hernandez P—15 (2011)
AO (Fly Outs):	Alfonso Soriano LF—205 (2006)
GO (Ground Outs):	Denard Span CF—236 (2013)
GO_AO (Ratio of GO to AO):	Wilson Ramos—2.13 (2015)
NP (Number of Pitches):	Adam Dunn—2909 (2009)
PA (Plate Appearances):	Alfonso Soriano—728 (2006)

Category	Statistic	Player
BA (Batting Avg.)	.289	Bryce Harper OF
OBP (On Base %)	.384	Bryce Harper OF
SLG (Slugging %)	.517	Bryce Harper OF
OPS (OBP + SLG)	.902	Bryce Harper OF
H (Hits)	1412	Ryan Zimmerman IF
2B (Doubles)	320	Ryan Zimmerman IF
3B (Triples)	28	Ian Desmond
RBI (Runs Batted In)	783	Ryan Zimmerman IF
R (Runs)	733	Ryan Zimmerman IF
HR (Home Runs)	200	Ryan Zimmerman IF
BB (Bases on Balls)	510	Ryan Zimmerman IF
IBB (Intentional Walks)	40	Ryan Zimmerman IF
HBP (Hit By Pitch)	53	Danny Espinosa 2B
SB (Stolen Bases)	122	Ian Desmond SS
KO (Strikeouts)	983	Ryan Zimmerman IF

Category	Statistic	Player
CS (Caught Stealing)	37	Ian Desmond SS
XBH (Extra Base Hits)	539	Ryan Zimmerman IF
SAC (Sacrifice Bunts)	43	Jordan Zimmermann RHP
SF (Sacrifice Flies)	52	Ryan Zimmerman IF
TB (Total Bases)	2370	Ryan Zimmerman IF
GDP (Grounded into Double Play)	161	Ryan Zimmerman IF
GO (Ground Outs)	1428	Ryan Zimmerman IF
AO (Fly Outs)	1315	Ryan Zimmerman IF
NP (Number of Pitches)	22054	Ryan Zimmerman IF
PA (Plate Appearances)	5573	Ryan Zimmerman IF

HISTORY—A brief history of the WASHINGTON Nationals:

The Montreal Expos, an expansion franchise founded in 1969, moved to D.C. in 2005 to become the Washington Nationals. The team name comes from the former D.C. team, The Washington Senators, which officially used "Nationals" beginning in 1905 (even though it was an American League team). "Nationals" appeared on the uniforms for only two seasons and then was replaced by the "W" logo.

The Montreal Expos was the first MLB team located outside the U.S. They won their only division championship in the strike shortened season of 1981. Notable players with the Montreal Expos included Hall of Famers Gary Carter and Andre Dawson who are both in the HOF as Expos, as well as Randy Johnson, Pedro Martinez, and Tony Perez. HOFers Frank Robinson (2002-04) and Dick Williams (1977-81) were managers with the Expos.

The Montreal Expos were purchased by twenty-nine MLB franchise owners as a temporary fix in 2002, and they were the owners when it was moved to Washington D.C. in 2005. After a seventeen month search, the Nationals were sold to the group headed by developer Theodore N. Lerner for 450 million dollars in 2006.

HITS—Leaders Each Season

(Top Nats highlighted #1-2-3)

2005:	156	Jose Guillen RF
2006:	179	Alfonso Soriano LF (#3)
2007:	174	Ryan Zimmerman 3B
2008:	183	Cristian Guzman SS (#2)
2009:	178	Ryan Zimmerman 3B
2010:	161	Ryan Zimmerman 3B
2011:	158	Michael Morse 1B
2012:	163	Ryan Zimmerman 3B
2013:	170	Denard Span CF
2014:	184	Denard Span CF (#1)
2015:	172	Bryce Harper

Fun Fact: The MLB all-time single season record is held by Ichiro Suzuki RF (Mariners) with 262; the NL record is held by Lefty O'Doul OF (Phillies) with 254 in 1929.

HOME RUNS—Leaders Each Season (Top Nats highlighted 1-2-3)

2005:	24	Jose Guillen RF
2006:	46	Alfonso Soriano LF (#1)
2007:	24	Ryan Zimmerman 3B
2008:	13	Lastings Milledge CF
2009:	38	Adam Dunn 1B (Tied #3)
2010:	38	Adam Dunn 1B (Tied #3)
2011:	31	Michael Morse 1B
2012:	33	Adam LaRoche 1B

2013:	26	Ryan Zimmerman 3B
2014:	26	Adam LaRoche 1B
2015:	42	Bryce Harper (#2)

Fun Fact: The MLB single season HR record is held by Barry Bonds LF (Giants) with 73.

HOME RUNS—Walk off—Team Leaders

Ryan Zimmerman IF—10
Bryce Harper OF—3

WALK OFFS in 2015: Michael Taylor (September 4), Bryce Harper (May 9), Ryan Zimmerman (May 19), Yunel Escobar (April 21)

Fun Fact: Jim Thome (1991-2012 Indians, Phillies, etc.) has the most career walk off home runs with 13.

HOME RUNS—Painted Seats:

Before the 2015 season, the Nationals announced they would begin marking significant home runs by painting the seats where they landed a different color. This follows a tradition started by the SENATORS in the late 1960s when they marked the landing spots of Frank Howard's long home runs by painting the seats white. In a 2004 interview with the *Baltimore Sun,* Howard said Senators' manager Ted Williams' comment about this was as follows: "There are 20 white seats and 17,000 seats in the whole upper deck. You see those 16,980 (other) seats? Those are all the times the (guy) struck out."

The first six home runs to be commemorated with painted seats and a plaque by the Nats:

- Ryan Zimmerman's Walk Off HR—March 30, 2008

- Michael Morse's Red Porch HR—July 20, 2012

- Jayson Werth's Walk Off HR, NLDS Game 4—October 11, 2012 (plaque in the bullpen)

- Adam LaRoche's Third Level HR—April 5, 2014

- Bryce Harper's Third Level HR—April 9, 2014

- Bryce Harper's Third Level HR, NLDS Game 1—October 3, 2014

HITTING—Most AT BATS (AB)—
Leaders Each Season (#1-2-3 highlighted)

2005:	565	Brad Wilkerson CF
2006:	647, 614	Alfonso Soriano LF, (#2, 647) Ryan Zimmerman 3B (#3, 614)
2007:	653	Ryan Zimmerman 3B (#1)
2008:	579	Cristian Guzman SS
2009:	610	Ryan Zimmerman 3B
2010:	558	Adam Dunn 1B
2011:	584	Ian Desmond SS
2012:	594	Danny Espinosa 2B
2013:	610	Denard Span CF
2014:	613	Anthony Rendon 3B
2015:	583	Ian Desmond SS

Fun Fact: The single season record is held by Jimmy Rollins SS (Phillies) with 716 AB's in 2007.

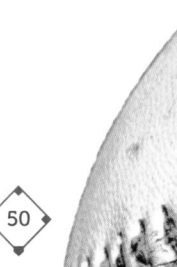

HITTING—# OF PITCHES (NP)—
Leaders Each Season *(#1-2-3 Nat highlighted)*

Year	NP	Player
2005	2248	Nick Johnson 1B
2006	2856	Alfonso Soriano LF (#3)
2007	2893	Ryan Zimmerman 3B (#2)
2008	2332	Lastings Milledge CF
2009	2909	Adam Dunn 1B (#1)
2010	2663	Adam Dunn 1B
2011	2835	Jayson Werth RF
2012	2616	Adam LaRoche 1B
2013	2540	Ryan Zimmerman 3B
2014	2710	Anthony Rendon 3B
2015	2682	Bryce Harper RF

Fun Fact: Ricky Gutierrez SS (Astros) is credited with the longest modern day at-bat, 20 pitches, against Bartolo Colon in 1998. On average, players face about 4 pitches per at-bat. The single season leader in number of pitches seen is Bobby Abreu RF (Phillies) with 3,168 in 2005; Mike Trout CF (Angels) is second with 3,136 in 2014.

HITTING—TOTAL PLATE APPEARANCES
(PA)—Leaders Each Season *(#1-2-3 highlighted)*

Year	PA	Player
2005:	661	Brad Wilkerson LF
2006:	728	Alfonso Soriano LF (#1)
2007:	722	Ryan Zimmerman 3B (#2)
2008:	612	Cristian Guzman SS
2009:	694	Ryan Zimmerman 3B (#3)
2010:	648	Adam Dunn 1B
2011:	658	Danny Espinosa 2B

2012:	658	Danny Espinosa 2B
2013:	662	Denard Span CF
2014:	683	Anthony Rendon 3B
2015:	654	Bryce Harper RF

Fun Fact: Jimmy Rollins SS (Phillies) holds the record for most total plate appearances with 778 in 2007.

HIT BY PITCH (HBP)—Leaders
Each Season *(#1-2-3 highlighted)*

Year	HBP	Player
2005	19	Jose Guillen RF (tied #1)
2006	13	Nick Johnson 1B
2007	8	Ryan Church LF
2008	14	Lastings Milledge CF (#2)
2009	9	Willie Harris LF
2010	10	Nyger Morgan CF
2011	19	Danny Espinosa 2B (tied #1)
2012	13	Danny Espinosa 2B (#3)
2013	5	Ian Desmond SS
2014	12	Danny Espinosa 2B
2015	8	Yunel Escobar IF

Fun Fact: Since 1900, the record for HBP is held by Ron Hunt 2B (Expos) who was hit 50 times in 1971.

18 INNINGS—Nats Longest Game: Six hours, thirty-four minutes

NLDS Game 2 on October 4, 2014—Nationals @ Giants

Giants finally won 2-1 after six hours and thirty-four minutes, the longest postseason game in history by time, and tied for the longest in innings.

Jordan Zimmermann came within one out of a shutout before being lifted, and allowed just three singles and one walk. Anthony Rendon hit an RBI single in the third; the Giants tied it up on Pablo Sandoval's double of Storen in the 9th. The Giants hero was Brandon Belt who hit the go ahead solo home run off Tanner Roark in the top of the 18th. Asdrubal Cabrera and Matt Williams were ejected in the 10th.

9 INNINGS—Longest Home Game: Four hours, fifty-three minutes

Wednesday, September 27, 2007 versus Phillies (loss)

9 INNINGS—Shortest Home Game: Two hours

Saturday, June 6, 2009 versus Mets

5 INNINGS—Shortest Abbreviated Home Game: One hour, thirty-seven minutes

Thursday, June 4, 2009 versus Giants

The second game of a double header (due to rain cancellation the previous day when Randy Johnson was supposed to get his 300th win); Johnson got his 300th in game 1. Giants won both games. Long day on the shortest game day.

Fun Fact: In 2015, the average length of a game in MLB was 3.01 hours, down from 3.13 in 2014, according to baseballprospectus.com.

IBB: Intentional Bases on Balls (Hitters) —Leaders Each Season (#1-2-3 highlighted):

Year	IBB	Player
2005	9	Brad Wilkerson LF
2006	16, 15	Alfonso Soriano LF (tied #1), Nick Johnson 1B (tied #2)
2007	7	Brian Schneider C
2008	4	Dmitri Young 1B
2009	16	Adam Dunn 1B (tied #1)
2010	10	Adam Dunn 1B (tied #3)
2011	8	Wilson Ramos C
2012	8	Ryan Zimmerman 3B
2013	10	Adam LaRoche 1B (tied #3)
2014	9	Adam LaRoche 1B
2015	15	Bryce Harper RF (tied #2)

Fun Fact: The single season record is held by Barry Bonds with 120 in 2004. In MLB history, only six players have been intentionally walked with the BASES LOADED. The reason for this would be the pitching team is leading by four runs or less late in the game and a feared hitter is at the plate. The six: Abner Dalrymple (1881), Nap Lajoie (1901), Del Bissonette (1928), Bill Nicholson (1944), Barry Bonds (1998), and Josh Hamilton (2008). In each case, the pitching team went on to win the game.

IBB: Intentional Bases on Balls Given up by Nats PITCHER—Leaders Each Season *(#1 highlighted):*

2005:	14	Livan Hernandez RHP (tied #1)
2006:	14	Ramon Ortiz (tied #1)
2007:	4	Tim Redding RHP, Jon Rauch RHP, Saul Rivera RHP, Jason Simontacchi RHP
2008:	7	Joel Hanrahan RHP
2009:	7	Jason Bergmann RHP
2010:	8	Miguel Batista RHP
2011:	6	Livan Hernandez RHP
2012:	5	Edwin Jackson RHP
2013:	3	Craig Stammen RHP, Zach Duke LHP
2014:	6	Jerry Blevins LHP
2015:	6	Blake Treinen RHP

Fun Fact: The single season record for IBB given up by a pitcher is held by Gene Garber (Phillies) with 24 in 1974.

INFIELD (1B, 2B, SS, 3B)—

BASIC STARTING INFIELD BY YEAR:

2005: Nick Johnson-Jose Vidro-Cristian Guzman-Vinny Castilla

2006: Nick Johnson-Jose Vidro-Royce Clayton-Ryan Zimmerman

2007: Dmitri Young-Ronnie Belliard-Felipe Lopez-Ryan Zimmerman

2008: Aaron Boone-Felipe Lopez-Cristian Guzman-Ryan Zimmerman

2009: Nick Johnson-Anderson Hernandez-Cristian Guzman-Ryan Zimmerman

2010: Adam Dunn-Adam Kennedy-Ian Desmond-Ryan Zimmerman

2011: Michael Morse-Danny Espinosa-Ian Desmond-Ryan Zimmerman

2012: Adam LaRoche-Danny Espinosa-Ian Desmond-Ryan Zimmerman

2013: Adam LaRoche-Anthony Rendon-Ian Desmond-Ryan Zimmerman

2014: Adam LaRoche-Danny Espinosa-Ian Desmond-Anthony Rendon

2015: Ryan Zimmerman-Danny Espinosa-Ian Desmond-Yunel Escobar

IMMACULATE (Perfect) INNING: 9 Pitches—9 Strikes—3 Outs

Jordan Zimmermann—May 6, 2011: versus Florida Marlins, struck out Giancarlo Stanton, Greg Dobbs, and John Buck in the second inning.

Fun Fact: There have been only eighty IMMACULATE INNINGS in MLB. Sandy Koufax did it three times! Lefty Grove, Nolan Ryan, and Randy Johnson did it twice. (baseball almanac.com)

IRONMEN of the Nats:

Year	Games Played	Player
2005	148	Brad Wilkerson LF
2006	159	Alfonso Soriano LF
2007	162, 161	Ryan Zimmerman 3B (#1, 162, perfect!), Austin Kearns RF (#2, 161)
2008	140	Willie Harris
2009	159	Adam Dunn 1B
2010	158	Adam Dunn 1B
2011	158	Danny Espinosa 2B
2012	160	Danny Espinosa 2B (#3)
2013	158	Ian Desmond SS
2014	154	Ian Desmond SS
2015	156	Ian Desmond SS

Fun Fact: The record for most games in a season is held by Maury Wills SS/LF (Dodgers) with 165 in 1962 (Dodgers and Giants were tied for first place in the NL, and played a three game tie breaker, thus 165 games). This was the first 162 game season for the NL (with addition of Houston Colt .45s and Mets); the AL started 162 games the year before.

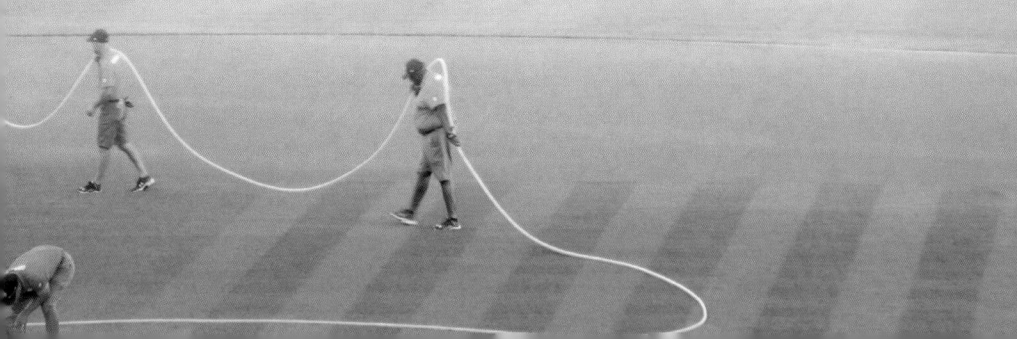

IRONMEN of the NATS: Most Games by
CATCHERS—Leaders Each Season *(#1-2-3 highlighted)*

Year	Games Played	Player
2005	116	Brian Schneider
2006	124	Brian Schneider (#3)
2007	129	Brian Schneider (#1)
2008	90	Jesus Flores
2009	90	Josh Bard
2010	111	Ivan Rodriguez
2011	113	Wilson Ramos
2012	83	Jesus Flores
2013	79	Kurt Suzuki
2014	88	Wilson Ramos
2015	125	Wilson Ramos (#2)

Fun Fact: Ted Simmons (Cardinals) holds the single season record, having caught 161 games in 1972.

IRONMEN of the NATS:

STARTING PITCHERS MOST INNINGS PITCHED—LEADERS EACH SEASON (#1-2-3 HIGHLIGHTED)		
2005:	246.1	Livan Hernandez RHP(#1)
	217.0	Estaban Loiza (#3)
2006:	190.2	Ramon Ortiz RHP
2007:	167.0	Matt Chico LHP
2008:	182.0	John Lannan LHP
2009:	206.1	John Lannan LHP
2010:	211.2	Livan Hernandez RHP
2011:	184.2	John Lannan LHP

2012:	199.1	Gio Gonzalez LHP
2013:	213.1	Jordan Zimmermann RHP
2014:	215.0	Stephen Strasburg RHP
2015:	228.2	Max Scherzer RHP (#2)

Fun Fact: The MLB all-time single season record (after 1900) is held by Ed Walsh (White Sox) with 464.0 innings in 1908. In more recent times, Wilbur Wood (White Sox), a left-handed knuckleballer, pitched 359.1 innings in 1973.

IRONMEN of the NATS:

RELIEVERS WITH THE MOST GAMES (#1-2-3 HIGHLIGHTED)

2005:	79	Gary Majewski RHP (#3)
2006:	85	Jon Rauch RHP (tied #2)
2007:	88	Jon Rauch RHP (#1)
	85	Saul Rivera RHP (tied #2)
2008:	76	Saul Rivera RHP
2009:	63	Ron Villone LHP
2010:	78	Tyler Clippard RHP
2011:	73	Drew Storen RHP
2012:	74	Tyler Clippard RHP
2013:	72	Tyler Clippard RHP
2014:	75	Tyler Clippard RHP
2015:	60	Blake Treinen RHP

Fun Fact: The pitcher with the most single season games is Mike Marshall (Dodgers) with 106 in 1974; he won the Cy Young Award that year. Overall, "Iron Mike" Marshall ranks #1 (106 in 1974—Dodgers), tied at #5 (92 games in 1973—Expos) and tied at #8 (90 games in 1979—Twins). In 1974, he also set the MLB record for most consecutive team games with a relief appearance with thirteen.

is for...

JERSEY NUMBERS:

Max Scherzer: Scherzer wore 37 (Strasburg's number) with the Tigers, so he selected 31, his number at University of Missouri (M I Z...Z O U).

Bryce Harper: Reportedly a Mickey Mantle fan thanks to his father, Harper decided to have a number that added up to 7 (34) if 7 was not available.

Stephen Strasburg: Strasburg wears the same number (37) he had at San Diego State University.

Jordan Zimmermann: Zimmermann wore 17 at University of Wisconsin—Stevens Point, and his number 23 Blue Devils American Legion jersey was retired in 2013. We could not locate a story on his Nats 27 jersey number (maybe what the Nats gave him?)

Danny Espinosa: Espinosa was given 18 by the team in 2012 but changed to number 8, which was his number pre major league.

Ian Desmond: Desmond changed his number from 6 to 20 in 2012. He was given 6 by the Nats but requested a change to 20 to honor former Nats manager Frank Robinson.

Ryan Zimmerman: In spring training 2006, he changed his number from 25 (what the Nats gave him originally) to 11, his number in college (UVA).

Wilson Ramos: Ramos switched from 3 to 40 in 2013; it appears he thought he was having bad luck with 3, and 40 was a good luck number in winter ball.

Roger Bernadina: Former Nat Bernadina gave his number 2 to Denard Span in January 2013 since Span had worn that number throughout his career; Bernadina took 33.

Fun Fact: The first MLB player to have his number retired was Lou Gehrig (4) in 1939. The most retired numbers are 4 and 5 (worn by Joe DiMaggio among others), retired by eight teams.

Some other famous retired jersey numbers 1 through 10:

#1	Ozzie Smith, Cardinals SS
#2	Charlie Gehringer, Tigers 2B and Nellie Fox, White Sox 2B
#3	Babe Ruth, Yankees OF/P
#4	Lou Gehrig, 1B and Duke Snider, Brooklyn Dodgers OF
#5	Joe DiMaggio, OF and Johnny Bench, Reds C
#6	Stan Musial, Cardinals OF/1B
#7	Mickey Mantle, Yankees OF
#8	Cal Ripken, Orioles SS
#9	Ted Williams, Red Sox OF
#10	Phil Rizzuto, Yankees SS and Chipper Jones, Braves 3B

Another fun fact: The only jersey number retired by all of MLB (in 1997) is #42 which belonged to Jackie Robinson 2B (Dodgers).

1. #17—Kris Bryant, Cubs 3B

2. #40—Madison Bumgarner, Giants P

3. #28—Buster Posey, Giants C/1B

4. #22—Clayton Kershaw, Dodgers P

5. #27—Mike Trout, Angels CF

6. #34—Bryce Harper, Nationals RF

JINXES and SUPERSTITIONS

JINXES: THE FAMOUS SPORTS ILLUSTRATED COVER JINX:

Some blame the October 1, 2012 SI cover, which highlighted the Nationals and Orioles, for the stunning Nats loss to the Cardinals in the first round of the playoffs (NLDS game five!). This cover has an Orioles photo alongside a banner stating, "Washington/Baltimore: The Unlikely Sports Capital," and highlights an article inside, "The Rogue Genius of Davey Johnson." It is also interesting that the same cover highlighted a Redskins article: "RG3: Change You Can Believe In"

The SI Baseball Preview regionals issue on April 1, 2013, which featured Nats pitcher Stephen Strasburg on the cover, predicted the Nats would win the World Series. This obviously did not work out. The magazine also picked them to win in 2014 (no cover), and then featured Bryce Harper and Max Scherzer on a regional MLB preview for 2015 predicting the Nats #1 in the NL East, first overall in the NL and losing to the Indians in the World Series.

Bryce Harper appeared on the cover in February 2013, and there was the Strasburg phenom issue in 2010… no direct damage there, but let's encourage SI to put the METS and BRAVES on their covers in the future.

A NEW JINX THEORY: The "Curse of Teddy":

An October 2, 2015 article in the Washington Post by Nats fan Mike Tidwell speculates that letting TEDDY ROOSEVELT win on October 3, 2012 may have caused a curse for the Washington Nationals. This jinx seems like a stretch, or maybe a desire to find an excuse for what has happened since by conjuring up a "Curse of the Bambino" or "Billy Goat" (Red Sox and Cubs). What do you think?

Nats Lineup Card

The Nats coaches apparently have both a superstition and competition when it comes to delivering the lineup card, according to James Wagner of the Washington Post (September 19, 2014).

As you know, before every game, a coach or the manager of each team delivers the lineup cards to the umpiring crew at home plate just before the game starts. Who delivers it is not a random choice: if you delivered and the Nats won, you will deliver again…that is, until a loss. At the time of this article, Matt WILLIAMS had the best luck, initiating a ten game winning streak, which included five walk offs in a six game span!

It is only fitting that the manager has the best record….

Banana and Mayo Sandwich (!)

Matt LeCroy, the Nats bullpen coach, eats a banana and mayo sandwich when the team needs a win. This is an "in a rut only" lucky sandwich charm: "You can't go to it all the time," he said. "If you go to it too much, it doesn't work." (James Wagner, Washington Post, June 9, 2014)

Maneki neko Figurine

A golden cat figurine, the Maneki neko is a Japanese good luck charm purchased for eight dollars by catcher Jose Lobaton in D.C.'s Chinatown. The Maneki neko has a left arm that swings like a pendulum. Positioned on the bat rack in the visitor's dugout, it did not work very well. Lobaton moved it, and—voila—a rally for 3 runs. That was in 2014, we are not sure how the cat is doing in 2015. (see Washington Post article, Adam Kilgore, October 7, 2014)

Fun Facts: Superstitions are big in sports and MLB. Some examples: Chipper Jones 3B (Braves) reportedly played computer solitaire until 6:55 every night of a game for good luck. Routines in the batter's box are pretty common, with the elaborate ritual of Nomar Garciaparra SS (Red Sox) being kind of famous. Torii Hunter OF (Twins) cleans his shoes before every game with Mr. Bubble spray. Jonny Gomes OF (Red Sox) said for clothing that comes in twos (socks, shoes), he always puts the right ones on first. Ty Cobb OF (Tigers) always swung three bats while on deck. Connie Mack (HOF manager of the Philadelphia Athletics) carried a chestnut from his family farm. Frank Chance 1B/Mgr (Cubs) insisted on riding in berth or stateroom #13 on train rides. John McGraw (Mgr) thought that a Giants wannabee, Charley Faust, (who was a bit off balance) brought luck to the team in 1911 and let him stick around, sitting on the bench and helping out…until they lost the World Series that year to the Philadelphia Athletics.

KO: STRIKEOUTS by HITTERS—
Leaders Each Season *(#1-2-3 Highlighted)*

2005:	147	Brad Wilkerson LF
2006:	160	Alfonso Soriano LF
2007:	125	Ryan Zimmerman 3B
2008:	96	Lastings Milledge CF
2009:	177	Adam Dunn 1B
2010:	199	Adam Dunn 1B (#1)
2011:	166	Danny Espinosa 2B
2012:	189	Danny Espinosa 2B (#2)
2013:	145	Ian Desmond SS
2014:	183	Ian Desmond SS
2015:	187	Ian Desmond SS (#3)

Fun Fact: the MLB all-time single season record for KO's is held by Mark Reynolds 3B (Diamondbacks) with 223 in 2009, and Adam Dunn DH (White Sox) is a close second with 222 in 2012.

KO: STRIKEOUTS LOOKING (L/SO)—

HITTERS—HIGHEST AND LOWEST LEADERS EACH SEASON BY %
(HIGHEST AND LOWEST PERCENTAGES HIGHLIGHTED)

Year	LS/O (Highest)	Player (# L/SO)	LS/O (Lowest)	Player
2005	39.1%	Nick Johnson 1B (34)	14.6%	Brian Schneider C
2006	39.4%	Nick Johnson 1B (39)	7.5%	Brian Schneider C
2007	38.2%	Ryan Zimmerman 3B (44)	14.0%	Ryan Church LF
2008	36.5%	Austin Kearns RF (23)	12.8%	Jesus Flores C
2009	38.7%	Willie Harris LF (24)	21.5%	Elijah Dukes CF
2010	41.2%	Josh Willingham LF (35)	15.2%	Ivan Rodgriguez C
2011	39.7%	Ryan Zimmerman 3B (29)	17.5%	Michael Morse 1B
2012	32.6%	Steve Lombardozzi 2B (15)	19.3%	Jayson Werth RF
2013	43.5%	Anthony Rendon 3B (30)	20.2%	Bryce Harper LF
2014	36.9%	Denard Span CF (24)	18.0%	Danny Espinosa 2B
2015	37.1%	Anthony Rendon 2B (26)	12.3%	Danny Espinosa 2B

Number wise, TOP FIVE NATS who had the most STRIKEOUTS LOOKING (#1 highlighted):

1. 54—Jayson Werth RF (33.8%) 2011
2. 53—Ian Desmond SS (38.1%) 2011
3. 53—Adam Dunn 1B (29.9%) 2009
4. 50—Ian Desmond SS (26.4%) 2015
5. 48—Ryan Zimmerman 3B (36.1%) 2013

Fun Fact: In 2014, the NL average percentage of L/SO was 24.4%. The MLB batting leader in 2014, Jose Altuve (Astros), struck out looking seventeen times (32.1%)—total strikeouts was fifty-three. On the other end in 2014, Chris Davis (Orioles) had fifty-six L/SO (32.4%)—total strikeouts was 117.

KO: STRIKEOUTS by PITCHERS—
Leaders Each Season *(#1-2-3 highlighted)*

2005:	185	John Patterson RHP
2006:	104	Ramon Ortiz RHP
2007:	94	Matt Chico LHP
2008:	120	Tim Redding RHP
2009:	92	Jordan Zimmermann RHP
2010:	114	Livan Hernandez RHP
2011:	124	Jordan Zimmermann RHP
2012:	207	Gio Gonzalez #3 LHP
2013:	192	Gio Gonazalez LHP
2014:	242	Stephen Strasburg (#2) RHP
2015:	276	Max Scherzer (#1) RHP
		(222 Swinging, 37 Looking) (#2 in MLB behind Dodger's Clayton Kershaw)

Fun Fact: the MLB all-time single season record is held by Nolan Ryan (Angels) with 383 in 1973; the NL record is held by Sandy Koufax (Dodgers) with 382 in 1965.

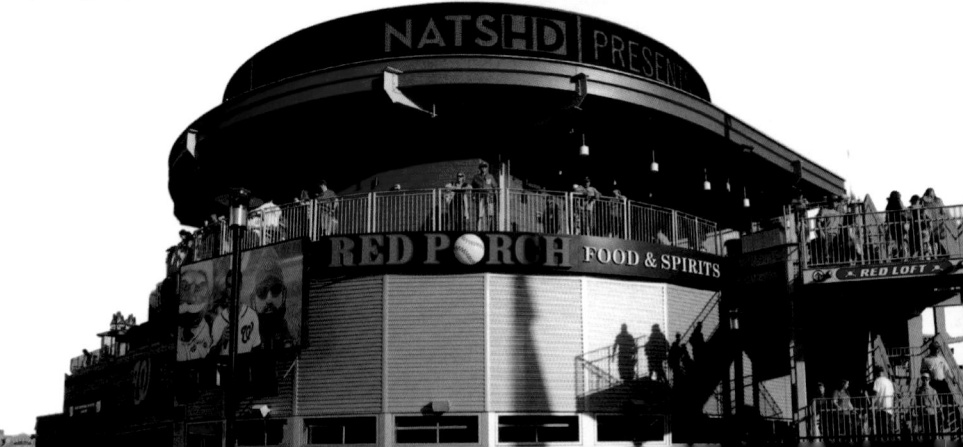

KO/9: Strikeouts per nine innings

Year	KO/9	Player
2005	8.39	John Patterson RHP
2006	5.67	Tony Armas RHP
2007	5.07	Matt Chico LHP
2008	6.71	Odalis Perez LHP
2009	3.88	John Lannan LHP
2010	4.85	Livan Hernandez RHP
2011	6.92	Jordan Zimmermann RHP
2012	9.35	Gio Gonzalez LHP (#1 in NL)
2013	9.39	Stephen Strasburg RHP (#3)
2014	10.13	Stephen Strasburg RHP (#2) (#2 in NL)
2015	10.86	Max Scherzer RHP (#1) (#3 in MLB)

Fun Fact: Randy Johnson (Diamondbacks) holds the single season record for K/9 with 13.4099 in 2001; Pedro Martinez (Red Sox) is second (13.2047 in 1999), and Kerry Wood (Cubs) ranks third (12.5820).

K/BB: Strikeout to walk ratio—

2005:	3.15	Esteban Loiza RHP
2006:	1.63	Ramon Ortiz RHP
2007:	1.20	Matt Chico LHP
2008:	1.63	John Lannan LHP
2009:	1.31	John Lannan LHP
2010:	1.78	Livan Hernandez RHP
2011:	4.00	Jordan Zimmermann RHP
2012:	2.72	Gio Gonzalez LHP
2013:	4.87	Dan Haren RHP

2014:	6.28	Jordan Zimmermann RHP (#2) (#2 in NL),
	5.63	Stephen Strasburg RHP (#3) (#3 in NL)
2015:	8.12	Max Scherzer (#1) RHP (#1 in MLB)

Fun Fact: The single season K/BB record is held by Phil Hughes (Twins) with 11.6250 in 2014.

KO%: PITCHER STRIKEOUT %—

STARTERS—LEADERS EACH SEASON (MINIMUM 150 INNINGS) (#1-2-3 HIGHLIGHTED)

2005:	22.6%	John Patterson RHP
2006:	14.0%	Tony Armas RHP
2007:	12.6%	Matt Chico LHP
2008:	16.7%	Odalis Perez LHP
2009:	10.2%	John Lannan LHP
2010:	12.7%	Livan Hernandez RHP
2011:	18.7%	Jordan Zimmermann RHP
2012:	25.2%	Gio Gonzalez LHP (#3 in NL)
2013:	26.1%	Stephen Strasburg RHP (#3) (#3 in NL)
2014:	27.9%	Stephen Strasburg RHP (#2) (#2 in NL)
2015:	30.7%	Max Scherzer RHP (#1)

Fun Fact: In the modern era, the single season leader (starters) in K% is Pedro Martinez (Red Sox) with 37.5% in 1999; Randy Johnson (Diamondbacks) is close behind with 37.4% in 2001. In 2014, the MLB leader in K% (starters) was Clayton Kershaw (Dodgers) with 31.9%; in 2013, it was Yu Darvish (Rangers) with 32.9%.

KO%: *RELIEF PITCHER STRIKEOUT %—*

1. 31.6% — *Tyler Clippard,* RHP 2011
2. 29.6% — *Tyler Clippard,* RHP 2010
3. 29.5% — *Tyler Clippard,* RHP 2014
4. 29.4% — *Drew Storen,* RHP 2015
5. 27.4% — *Tyler Clippard,* RHP 2012

Fun Fact: The single season leader among relievers is Aroldis Chapman (Reds) with 52.5% in 2013; second is Craig Kimbrel (Braves) with 50.2% in 2012.

LEADERS—#1 Nats Leading in MLB and National League

NATS WHO HAVE RANKED #1 in MLB:

Bryce Harper RF

- —OPS (on base plus slugging %)—1.109 (2015)
- —SLG (slugging %)—.649 (2015)
- —OBP (on base %)—.460 (2015)
- —WAR (wins above replacements)—9.5 (2015)
- —RUNS Created—161 (2015)

Max Scherzer RHP

- —CG (complete games)—4 (tied) (2015)
- —SHO (shutouts)—3 (tied) (2015)
- —KO/BB (ration strikeouts/base on balls)—8.118

Gio Gonzales LHP

- —HR/FB (home runs to foul balls)—5.9%

Chad Cordero RHP

—Saves—47 (2005)

Livan Hernandez RHP

—Innings Pitched—246.1 (2005)
—Livo was also #1 in Games Started (35), #1 in hits (268), and #1 in Batters Faced (1,065)

Ryan Zimmerman IF

—Games Played—162 (tied) (2007)

Jon Rauch RHP

—Games Played (Pitcher)—88 (2007)

Denard Span CF

—Triples—11 (2013)

Gio Gonzalez LHP

—Wins—21 (2012)
—Also #1 in Home Runs per 9 IP (0.406), and in Fielding Independent Pitching (FIP) (2.82)

Jordan Zimmermann RHP

—Shutouts —2 (tied) (2013)

Henry Rodriguez RHP

—Wild Pitches—14 (2011)

NATS WHO HAVE RANKED #1 in NL:

Bryce Harper OF
—Runs—118 (2015)
—HR (home runs)—42 (tied) (2015)
—AT BATS per HR—12.4 (2015)

Max Scherzer RHP
—KO's per 9 IP—11.643 (2015)
—Batters Faced—899 (2015)

Ian Desmond SS
—Errors—27 (2015)

Alfonso Soriano LF
—Extra Base Hits—89 (2006)

Ramon Ortiz RHP
—Losses—16 (2006)

Danny Espinosa 2B
—Hit By Pitch (tied)—19 (2011)
—Strikeouts—189 (2012)

Anthony Rendon 3B
—Runs Scored—111 (2014)

Denard Span CF
—Hits (tied)—184 (2014)

Jordan Zimmermann RHP
—Wins (tied)—19 (2013)

Stephen Strasburg RHP
—Strikeouts—242 (2014)
—Games Started—34 (2014)

Jordan Zimmermann RHP
—Bases on Balls per Innings Pitched—1.307 (2014)

LINE UP: Nats Main LEAD-OFF Hitters by Season:

Year	Player	# of Games
2005	Brad Wilkerson OF	136
2006	Alfonso Soriano OF	131
2007	Felipe Lopez 2B	103
2008	Felipe Lopez 2B	42
2009	Christian Guzman SS	49
2010	Nyger Morgan CF	104
2011	Roger Bernadina OF	52
2012	Steve Lombardozzi 2B/OF	58
2013	Denard Span CF	134
2014	Denard Span CF	144
2015	Denard Span CF, Michael Taylor	61 (Span) 31 (Taylor)

LINE UP: Nats Main CLEAN UP Hitters (4 Hole) by Season:

Year	Player	# of Games
2005	Jose Guillen OF	64
2006	Nick Johnson 1B	112
2007	Dmitri Young 1B	106
2008	Lastings Milledge CF, Austin Kearns OF	25
2009	Adam Dunn 1B	142
2010	Adam Dunn 1B	125
2011	Michael Morse 1B	82
2012	Adam LaRoche 1B	105
2013	Adam LaRoche 1B	49
2014	Adam LaRoche 1B	134
2015	Bryce Harper OF	59

LINE UPS:

- **2005:** Wilkerson-Guzman-Vidro-Guillen-Johnson-Castilla-Sledge-Schneider-Hernandez

- **2006:** Watson-Vidro-Guillen-Johnson-Soriano-Zimmerman-Clayton-Schneider-Hernandez

- **2007:** Lopez-Guzman-Zimmerman-Kearns-Young-Schneider-Church-Logan-Patterson

- **2008:** Guzman-Milledge-Zimmerman-Johnson-Kearns-LoDuca-Dukes-Belliard-Perez

- **2009:** Milledge-Guzman-Zimmerman-Dunn-Johnson-Kearns-Belliard-Flores-Lannan

- **2010:** Morgan-Harris-Zimmerman-Dunn-Willingham-Kennedy-Rodgriguez-Desmond-Lannan

- **2011:** Desmond-Werth-Zimmerman-LaRoche-Morse-Ankiel-Espinosa-Rodriguez-Hernandez

- **2012:** Desmond-Espinosa-Zimmerman-LaRoche-Werth-DeRosa-Bernadina-Ramos-Strasburg

- **2013:** Span-Werth-Harper-Zimmerman-LaRoche-Desmond-Espinosa-Ramos-Strasburg

- **2014:** Span-Zimmerman-Werth-Ramos-Harper-Desmond-LaRoche-Rendon-Strasburg

- **2015:** Taylor-Escobar-Harper-Zimmerman-Ramos-Desmond-Uggla-Moore-Scherzer

LEFTIES: NATS NOTABLE LEFTIES—PITCHERS

2005:	John Halama, Mike Stanton, Joey Eischen
2006:	Mike O'Connor, Mike Stanton, Billy Traber
2007:	Matt Chico, Mike Bascik, Ray King
2008:	John Lannan, Odalis Perez, Matt Chico
2009:	John Lannan, Ross Detwiler, Scott Olsen
2010:	John Lannan, Scott Olsen, Dout Slaten, Ross Detwiler
2011:	John Lannan, Sean Burnett, Tom Gorzelanny, Ross Detwiler
2012:	Gio Gonzalez, Ross Detwiler, Tom Gorzelanny, Zach Duke
2013:	Gio Gonzalez, Ross Detwiler, Fernando Abad, Zach Duke
2014:	Gio Gonzalez, Jerry Blevins, Ross Detwiler, Matt Thornton
2015:	Gio Gonzalez, Matt Thornton, Felipe Rivero, Sammy Solis

Note: What is a LOOGY?

A left handed specialist relief pitcher is sometimes called a LOOGY, which stands for Lefty One Out Guy, i.e. a pitcher who comes in to face just one left handed batter or two. Jesse OROSCO is an example of this kind of specialist.

LEFTIES: NATS NOTABLE LEFTIES—BATTERS

2005:	Brian Schneider, Nick Johnson, Brad Wilkerson
2006:	Brian Schneider, Nick Johnson
2007:	Brian Schneider, Ryan Church

2008:	Willie Harris, Nick Johnson, Ryan Langerhans
2009:	Nick Johnson, Willie Harris, Adam Dunn, Nyjer Morgan
2010:	Adam Dunn, Adam Kennedy, Nyjer Morgan, Roger Bernadina
2011:	Laynce Nix, Rick Ankiel, Roger Bernadina, Adam LaRoche
2012:	Adam LaRoche, Bryce Harper, Roger Bernadina, Rick Ankiel, Chad Tracy
2013:	Adam LaRoche, Bryce Harper, Denard Span, Roger Bernadina, Chad Tracy
2014:	Adam LaRoche, Bryce Harper, Denard Span, Nate McLouth
2015:	Bryce Harper, Clint Robinson, Matt den Dekker, Denard Span

Fun Fact: Left-handed hitters make up about 25% of MLB hitters (and 10% of the population), with about one third of those being "true lefties" and the others batting left but throwing right handed. Of the Nats 2015 lefties, Harper bats left and throws right; Robinson, Den Decker, and Span are left/left. Left handed batters are desirable based on the concept that hitters usually hit better against an opposite handed pitcher; pitchers are predominantly right handed, throwing between 70-75% of big league innings. They are less in demand in the field, traditionally occupying 1st base and outfield positions. Famous left handed hitters: Ted Williams, Babe Ruth, Ty Cobb, Ken Griffey, and Stan Musial.

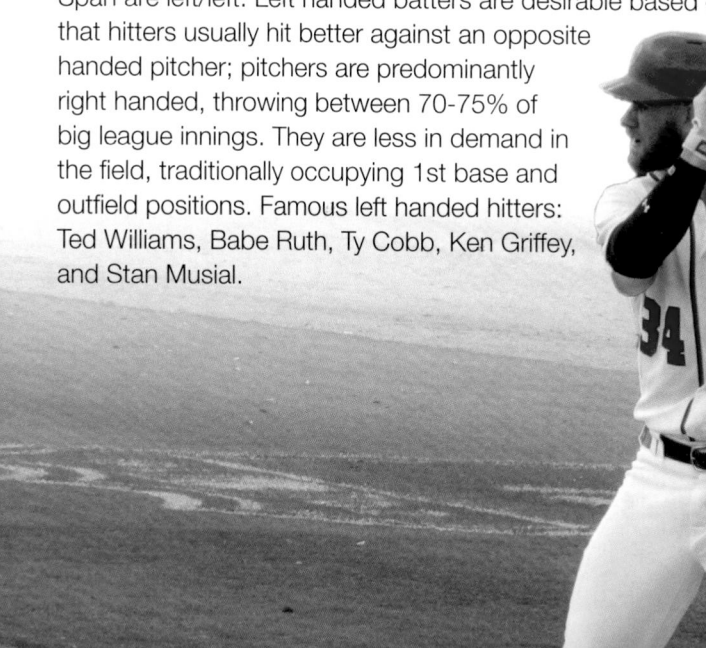

is for...

MAX! #31 MAD MAX SCHERZER—

A little bio:

- Scherzer is from St. Louis (Chesterfield), was drafted by the Cardinals in the 43rd round out of high school in 2003, but did not sign and attended the University of Missouri (Mizzou) instead. In 2006, he was drafted in the first round by the Diamondbacks (11th overall); he was the first Mizzou baseball player drafted in the first round.

- Scherzer made his debut against the Astros on April 29, 2008, and set the record for the number of consecutive batters retired (13) for a pitcher making his MLB debut as a reliever.

- Scherzer was traded to the Tigers in December 2009. In 2013, he became the first Tigers pitcher to start a season 12-0. He won the AL Cy Young Award in 2013 and was the AL wins leader in both 2013 and 2014.

- Scherzer is a three-time All-Star: twice with the Tigers and once as an All-Star with the Nats in 2015.

- Scherzer was signed by the Nationals to a seven-year, $210 million contract in January 2015.

- Scherzer throws four main pitches. In 2015, his pitching breakdown: 59.4% fastballs, 18.8% sliders, 13.2% changeups, 8.1% curveballs.

- Scherzer achieved a game score of 97 or more three times in 2015: 100 on June 14 vs. Milwaukee (no-hitter), 97 on July 20 vs. Pittsburgh (shutout), and 104 on October 3 vs. the Mets (no-hitter). e is the only pitcher with two 100s in a single season.

2015 was a career year for Scherzer—
take a look at the following stats:

#1 MLB

- **CG** (complete games) – 4
  (tied with Jake Arrieta/Cubs, Clayton Kershaw/Dodgers, and Madison BumgarnerGiants)

- **SHO** (shutouts) – 3
  (tied with Jake Arrieta/Cubs and Clayton Kershaw/Dodgers)

- **K/BB** (strikeouts/bases on balls) - 8.12
  #9 on the all-time list, after Ben Sheets (Brewers-2004) with 8.25.

#2 MLB

- **BB/9** (bases on balls per 9 innings) - 1.338
  #1 in 2015 was Bartolo Colon/Mets with 1.11

- **KO** (Strikeouts) – 276
  #1 in 2015 was Clayton Kershaw/Dodgers with 301.2

- **BB%** (bases on balls %) - 3.8
  #1 in 2015 was Bartolo Colon/Mets with 2.9%.

#3 MLB

- **K/BB%** (strikeout to walk %) - 26.9%

- **K/9** (strikeouts per 9) - 10.863

- **K%** (strikeout %) - 30.7

- **TBF** (Total Batters Faced) – 899

- **Pitcher's WAR** (wins above replacements) - 6.4 (tied)

#4 MLB

- **WHIP** (walks + hits per innings pitched) - 0.92

- **IP** (innings pitched) - 228.2

More Stats:

- BAA (batting average against): .205 (#5 MLB)

- First Pitch Strike %: 71.3 (#1 MLB)

- Swinging Strikeouts%: 15.3% (#4 MLB)

- Swing %: 55.2% (#2 MLB)

- Two no-hitters!

Career best numbers achieved in 2015 include: ERA (2.79), Strikeouts (276), WHIP (0.92), BB/9 (1.34), KO% (30.7), BB% (3.8%), Complete Games (4), and Shutouts (3).

Fun Fact: Max Scherzer has two different colored eyes. His right eye is blue while his left eye is brown, and it is very striking in his case. The condition is called heterochromia iridum. According to medicinenet.com, it affects about six people out of 1,000 (around 53,600 people in the U.S. per year), but in most of those cases, it is not noticeable. Scherzer's previous team, the Tigers, distributed a bobblehead featuring the correct eye colors. One other former MLB player was located with the condition: Michael Schwimer, who pitched for the Phillies 2011-12. Celebrities who have this condition include Kiefer Sutherland, Dan Aykroyd, Demi Moore and Tim McIlrath (lead singer of Rise Against).

M is for MASCOT Screech:

Screech, a bald eagle, was "hatched" on April 17, 2005 at the "Kids Opening Day" promotion at RFK Stadium. He was designed by nine year old fourth grade student in D.C., named Glenda Gutierrez. The original Screech had a "healthy" physique—rotund and fuzzy looking (great with the "belly" dancing). In 2009, Screech was given a more svelte, grown up (and athletic) look.

MINOR LEAGUE—Nats Minor League Team MASCOTS

SYRACUSE CHIEFS—Scooch and Pops (AAA, International league)

HARRISBURG SENATORS—Rascal (AA, Eastern League)

POTOMAC Nationals—Uncle Sam (Advanced A, Caroline League)

HAGERSTOWN SUNS—Woolie (a Giant Woolly Bear Caterpillar) (A, South Atlantic League

AUBURN DOUBLEDAYS—Abner, named after Abner Doubleday, the Civil War general and Auburn native credited with "inventing" the game of baseball (Short Season A, New York-Penn League)

MINOR LEAGUE AWARD HISTORY *(interesting to look at the past):*

Yellow Highlighted Names: Still with the Nats as of 2015 (minor or MLB)

BLUE Names: Made it to MLB/Nats (debut or more) but then changed teams (traded, etc.)

RED Names: Traded before moving up to MLB/Nats

2005: **Kory Casto IF** (Player of the Year), **Michael O'Connor LHP** (Pitcher of the Year). O'Connor last appeared in MLB for the Mets in 2011.

2006: **Kory Casto IF** (Player of the Year), **Zechry Zinicola RHP**

(Pitcher of the Year). Casto retired from baseball in 2010. Zinicola is possibly retired.

2007: **Justin Maxwell OF** (Player of the Year), **John Lannan LHP** (Pitcher of the Year). Maxwell was with the Giants in 2015; Lannan possibly retired in 2015.

2008: **Leonard Davis OF** (Player of the Year), **Jordan Zimmermann RHP** (Pitcher of the year). Davis is possibly retired.

2009: **Derek Norris C** (Player of the Year), **Brad Meyers RHP** (Pitcher of the Year). Norris played with the Padres in 2015, Meyers was released by the Nats in 2014.

2010: **Tyler Moore OF** (Player of the Year), **Tom Milone LHP** (Pitcher of the Year). Milone was traded to the Athletics in 2011, and was with the Twins in 2014 15.

2011: **Steve Lombardozzi IF** (Player of the Year), **Brad Peacock** (Pitcher of the Year). Lombardozzi may have retired; Peacock was traded to the Athletics in 2011, and then to the Astros.

2012: **Matthew Skole IF** (player of the Year), **Nathan Karns RHP** (Pitcher of the Year). Karns was traded to the Rays in 2014.

2013: **Billy Burns OF** (Player of the Year), **Taylor Jordan RHP** (Pitcher of the Year), **Tony Renda 2B** (Bob Boone Award for Leadership). Burns was traded to the Athletics in 2013 for Jeremy Blevins; Renda was traded to the Yankees in 2015 for David Carpenter.

2014: **Steven Souza Jr. OF** (Player of the Year), **Lucas Giolito RHP** (Pitcher of the Year), Wilmer Difo IF (Bob Boone Award for Leadership). Souza was traded to the Rays in 2014 in a three team trade, which brought pitcher Joe Ross to the Nats.

2015: **Jose Marmolejos 1B** (Player of the Year), **Austin Voth RHP** (Pitcher of the Year, Austen Williams RHP (Bob Boone Award for Leadership)

M is for MEMORIES—
A Short List of Amazing Nats Memories

- Opening Day 2005

- RFK metal stands (the stomping!) and hot chocolate

- Tailgating in RFK parking lot

- First Live President's Race on July 21, 2006

- Nats Park Opening Day March 22, 2008

- Zimmerman Walk off Home Run Opening Day (see above)

- Strasburg Debut June 8, 2010—14 strikeouts (franchise record)

- First Teddy Win—October 3, 2012 (final day of regular season)

- First Post Season NLDS vs Cardinals October 7 12, 2012

- Werth Walk off Home Run Game 4 NLDS October 11, 2012

- Jordan Zimmermann No-Hitter last day of 2014 season— September 28, 2014

- Steven Souza Diving Catch to Save Zimmermann No-Hitter (September 28, 2014)

- Max Scherzer No-Hitters—June 20, 2015 and October 3, 2015.

MANAGERS:
Welcome Dusty Baker!

Year	Manager	W-L
2005	Frank Robinson	81-81, last place NL East
2006	Frank Robinson	71-91, last place NL East
2007	Manny Acta	73-89, fourth place NL East
2008	Manny Acta	59-102, the worst record in MLB, last place NL East
2009	Manny Acta, Jim Riggleman	59 103, last place in NL East
2010	Jim Riggleman	69 93, last place NL East
2011	Jim Riggleman, John McLaren, Davey Johnson	80-81, third place NL East
2012	Davey Johnson	98-64, reached post season —NL Manager of the Year
2013	Davey Johnson	86-76, second place NL East
2014	Matt Williams	96-66, reached post season— NL Manager of the Year
2015	Matt Williams	83-79, second place NL East

Get to know the MANAGERS:

Johnnie B. "Dusty" Baker:

- Officially announced as the Nats new manager on November 5, 2015.

- Three-time NL Manager of the Year.

- Led the Giants to five ninety win seasons.

- Twenty seasons leading the Giants (1993-2002), Cubs (2003-06) and Reds (2008-13), seven trips to the postseason.

- As a player (OF), had nineteen seasons with the Braves (1968-75), Dodgers (1976-83), Giants (1984) and Athletics (1985-86); two time All-Star (1981, 1982), NLCS MVP in 1977, World Series Champion in 1981.

- Playing career numbers: .278 batting average, 242 home runs, 1,013 runs batted in.

- According to Wikipedia, he may have conducted the first ever "high five" (check it out).

Matt Williams:

- Came to the Nats from the Arizona Diamondbacks, where the last three seasons he served as the 3rd base coach.

- Former third baseman, retired as a player in 2003; final five seasons with the Diamondbacks.

- Five time All-Star, four Gold Gloves and four Silver Sluggers, ranked third all-time in homers for a third baseman (359) after Mike Schmidt and Chipper Jones.

- Only player to hit home runs in the World Series for three different teams (Diamondbacks, Indians, Giants).

- Native of Carson City, NV; his grandfather, OF Bert Griffith, played in six games for the 1924 Champion AL Nationals.

Davey Johnson:

- As a manager, won seven Division titles (including one for the Nats), one pennant ('86 Mets) and one World Series ('86 Mets).

- As a player, was starting second baseman for the Baltimore Orioles making his debut on April 13, 1965.

- Won four AL pennants and two World Series playing with the Orioles.

- Only player to have hit behind both Hank Aaron and Japan's all-time home run king, Sudaharu Oh.

- Retired to Florida, is working in commercial real estate.

John McLaren:

- Interim manager of the Nats in 2011, serving between Riggleman and Johnson. McLaren was previously manager for the Seattle Mariners.

- As of 2014, a professional scout for the Oakland Athletics.

Jim Riggleman:

- Named bench coach for the Nats in 2009.

- Picked up as manager for the 2010 and part of the 2011 season.

- As of 2014, third base coach for the Cincinnati Reds.

Manny Acta:

- Third base coach for the EXPOS under Frank Robinson 2002-05.

- First manager job with the Nationals in 2007.

- Managed the Cleveland Indians 2010-12, and is currently an ESPN baseball analyst.

Frank Robinson:

- Inaugural manager for the Nats, coming over with the EXPOS where he managed from 2002-04.

- Elected to the HOF in 1982 (as a player--OF), Robinson was an Oriole for two World Series championships (1966 and 1970).

- Won the coveted Triple Crown in 1966.

- 14 time All-Star and an MVP twice for two different leagues (1961 NL MVP, 1966 AL MVP), as well as the World Series MVP in 1966.

Note: The youngest manager to start a season with a club was Lou Boudreau. He was just 24 when he became the player manager of the Cleveland Indians in 1941.

N IS FOR **N**ICKNAMES

Chad Cordero— "The Chief"

The most famous nickname for the Nationals might be "The Chief" because of the way Chad Cordero won the hearts of Nats fans when he provided such an exciting season as the closer. In June 2005 he tied the major league record for saves in one month with fifteen, led the major leagues at the end of the season with forty-seven and struck out Ivan Rodriguez (future National) in the All-Star Game.

Roger Bernadina— "The Shark"

Bernadina's nickname is an interesting story according to an article by Dan Steinberg ("How Roger Bernadina Became the Shark" 06/30/2011). Two twenty something fans, Tyler Stoltenberg and Terry Cangelosi, decided to give Bernadina some well-deserved fan attention and thought a great nickname was in order. They happened to have shark hats for their job at a children's theater, plus they thought Bernadina looked like a shark hunting his prey when tracking down fly balls, so they picked "The Shark." After a short time, it caught on big time at Nationals Park (including shark jaw hand motions by the fans in the stands).

Other notable nicknames:

Michael Morse — **"The Beast"**

Adam Dunn — **"The Big Donkey"**

Wilson Ramos — **"The Buffalo"**

Jayson Werth — **"The Beard"** and maybe **"Were Werth"**

Anthony Rendon — **"Tony Two Bags"**

Max Scherzer — **"Mad Max"**

NATIONAL LEAGUE—short history

- The National League of Professional Baseball Clubs, known as the National League (NL), was formed on February 2, 1876, and is older than the American League

- NL Teams have won 47 of the 110 World Series games

- NL had eight teams for over sixty years, and expanded in 1960 to add the New York Mets and the Houston Colt .45's (Astros)— becoming ten teams

- Two more teams were added in 1969—San Diego Padres and Montreal Expos (Nats)—then twelve teams.

- In 1993, the NL expanded to fourteen teams with the addition of the Colorado Rockies and the Florida (Miami) Marlins, and the Arizona Diamondbacks in 1998 made fifteen. Also, the Milwaukee Brewers moved from the AL to the NL, adding up to sixteen.

- In 2013, the Astros moved to the AL West—minus one.

- NL and AL now have 3 Divisions, each with five teams, for a total of fifteen

- NL never adopted the "designated hitter" rule used by the AL

- Interleague games began in 1997. Before that, the two leagues played against each other only in exhibition games or the World Series.

NL EAST TEAMS:

Washington Nationals: 2 NL East Division Titles (2012, 2014)

New York Mets: 2 World Series titles (1969, 1969); 4 NL Pennants, 5 NL East Division Titles

Atlanta Braves: 3 World Series titles (1914, 1957, 1995); 17 NL Pennants, 12 NL East Division Titles

Miami Marlins: 2 World Series titles (1997, 2003); 2 NL Pennants

Philadelphia Phillies: 2 World Series titles (1980, 2008); 7 NL Pennants, 11 NL East Division Titles

NATIONAL LEAGUE EAST DIVISION CHAMPIONS—*POST SEASON*

2012 NLDS:

Washington Nationals (East Division Champions, 98-64) vs St. Louis Cardinals (Wild Card Game Winner, 88-74)

Game 1: Nats won, 3-2 (Busch Stadium)—WP Ryan Mattheus, LP Mitchell Boggs, SV Drew Storen

Game 2: Nats lost, 12-4 (Busch Stadium)—WP Lance Lynn, LP Jordan Zimmermann

Game 3: Nats lost 8-0 (Nationals Park)—WP Chris Carpenter, LP Edwin Jackson

Game 4: Nats won 2-1 (Nationals Park)—WP Drew Storen, LP Lance Lynn. Jayson Werth, on the 13th pitch, lined a home into left field, giving the Nats a 2-1 win.

Game 5: Nats lost 9-7 (Nationals Park) WP Jason Motte, LP Drew Storen. A painful loss for the Nats, who had expectations of moving on until giving up 4 runs in the 9th.

Cardinals win series 3-2.

Nats Top Stats in the 2012 NLDS:

Category	Statistic	Player
Batting Avg.	.381	Ryan Zimmerman 3B
OPS	1.078	Ryan Zimmerman 3B
OBP	.364	Ryan Zimmerman 3B
SLG	.714	Ryan Zimmerman 3B
Hits	8	Ryan Zimmerman 3B
RBI	4	Ryan Zimmerman 3B
Runs	4	Adam LaRoche 1B
ERA	4.5	Gio Gonzalez LHP
KOs	10	Gio Gonzalez LHP
Wins	1	Ryan Matheus RHP (1), Drew Storen RHP (1)

2014 NLDS:

Washington Nationals (East Division champion 96-66) vs the San Francisco Giants (Wild Card Winner, 88-74) October 3 7, 2014

Game 1: Nats lost 3-2 (Nationals Park)—WP Jake Peavy, LP Stephen Strasburg

Game 2: Nats lost 2-1 (Nationals Park)—18 Innings (SEE "Innings— longest game")—WP Yusmeiro Petit, LP Tanner Roark

Game 3: Nats won 4-1 (Giants AT&T Park) –WP Doug Fister, LP Madison Bumgarner

Game 4: Nats lost 3-2 (Giants AT&T Park)—WP Hunter Strickland, LP Matt Thornton

Giants won series 3 1.

Nats Top stats in 2014 NLDS:

Category	Statistic	Player
Batting Avg.	.368	Anthony Rendon 3B
OPS	1.251	Bryce Harper LF
OBP	.400	Anthony Rendon 3B
SLG	.882	Bryce Harper LF
Hits	7	Anthony Rendon 3B
RBI	4	Bryce Harper LF
Runs	4	Bryce Harper LF
ERA	1.04	Jordan Zimmermann RHP
KOs	6	Jordan Zimmermann RHP
Wins	1	Doug Fister RHP

is for...

OPENING DAY—
STARTING PITCHERS—Each Season

2005:	Livan Hernandez RHP
2006:	Livan Hernandez RHP
2007:	John Patterson RHP
2008:	Odalis Perez LHP
2009:	John Lannan LHP
2010:	John Lannan LHP
2011:	Livan Hernandez RHP
2012:	Stephen Strasburg RHP
2013:	Stephen Strasburg RHP
2014:	Stephen Strasburg RHP
2015:	Max Scherzer RHP

OFF-SPEED:
Livan Hernandez—An Appreciation

Livan defected from Cuba in 1995. He was a World Series champion and MVP in 1997 for the Florida Marlins. As a young starter, he had a mid 90s fastball, but changed to a finesse pitcher as he got older. His four seam fastball was the slowest among all MLB starters in the 2011 season, proving a significant challenge to most hitters. He had seven full seasons without making an error. "Livo" was a fan favorite and lifted Nats fans' spirits as he consistently frustrated our opponents inning after inning. Thanks, Livo!

OPS = OBP + SLUGGING:

OBP (On Base Percentage)—Leaders Each Season

(400+ PLATE APPEARANCES) (#1-2-3 HIGHLIGHTED):

Year	OBP	Player
2005	.408	Nick Johnson 1B (#3)
2006	.428	Nick Johnson 1B (#2)
2007	.378	Dimitri Young 1B
2008	.345	Cristian Guzman SS
2009	.398	Adam Dunn 1B
2010	.389	Josh Willingham LF
2011	.360	Michael Morse 1B
2012	.346	Ryan Zimmerman 3B
2013	.398	Jayson Werth RF
2014	.394	Jayson Werth RF
2015	.460	Bryce Harper RF (#1) (#1 in MLB)

Fun Fact: Best all-time MLB single season for OBP—Barry Bonds OF (Giants) with .609 in 2004.

Slugging Percentage—Leaders Each Season

Year	OBP	Player
2005	.479	Nick Johnson 1B
2006	.560	Alfonso Soriano LF (#2)
2007	.491	Dimitri Young 1B
2008	.442	Ryan Zimmerman 3B
2009	.529	Adam Dunn 1B
2010	.536	Adam Dunn 1B
2011	.550	Michael Morse 1B (#3)
2012	.511	Ian Desmond SS
2013	.532	Jayson Werth OF
2014	.473	Anthony Rendon 3B
2015	.649	Bryce Harper OF (#1) (#1 in MLB)

Fun Fact: Best all-time MLB single season slugging percentage—Barry Bonds OF (Giants) with .863 in 2001.

OPS (On Base plus Slugging %)—Leaders Each Season

Year	OBP	Player
2005	.887	Nick Johnson 1B
2006	.948	Nick Johnson 1B (#2)
2007	.869	Dimitri Young 1B
2008	.786	Cristian Guzman SS
2009	.928	Adam Dunn 1B
2010	.899	Ryan Zimmerman 3B
2011	.910	Michael Morse 1B
2012	.853	Adam LaRoche 1B
2013	.931	Jayson Werth OF (#3)
2014	.849	Jayson Werth OF
2015	1.109	Bryce Harper OF (#1) (#1 in MLB)

Fun Fact: Best all-time MLB single season OPS—Barry Bonds OF (Giants) with 1.4217 in 2004.

OUTFIELD COMBOS—

2005:	Marlon Byrd-Brad Wilkerson-Jose Guillen
2006:	Alfonso Soriano-Marlon Byrd-Jose Guillen
2007:	Ryan Church-Nook Logan-Austin Kearns
2008:	Willie Harris-Lastings Milledge-Austin Kearns
2009:	Josh Willingham-Willie Harris-Elijah Dukes
2010:	Josh Willingham-Nyger Morgan-Michael Morse
2011:	Laynce Nix-Rick Ankiel-Jayson Werth
2012:	Michael Morse-Bryce Harper-Jayson Werth
2013:	Bryce Harper-Denard Span-Jayson Werth
2014:	Bryce Harper-Denard Span-Jayson Werth
2015:	Jayson Werth-Michael Taylor-Bryce Harper

Owners of the Nationals:

When baseball moved to Washington D.C., the team (Expos) had been owned and operated by Major League Baseball since February 5, 2002. On May 4, 2006, MLB announced that they had awarded the Washington National franchise to a group of area businessmen led by developer Theodore (Ted) N. Lerner, ending a seventeen–month search. Lerner was selected over seven other bidders, and his ownership group of fourteen investors includes his son, Mark D. Lerner, who runs the franchise, and his sons in law, Edward L. Cohen and Robert K. Tanenbaum. According to Wikipedia, the Lerner family is the majority owner of the franchise, controlling over 90% of the shares.

Ted Lerner: Born in 1925, Lerner is a real estate developer and founder of the Lerner Enterprises company, reportedly the largest private landowner in the Washington D.C. area, with a wide portfolio of commercial, retail, residential, and hotel properties, as well as the Chelsea Piers in New York. The Lerner family is also a partner in Monumental Sports & Entertainment, which owns the NHL Washington Capitals, WNBA Washington Mystics, NBA Washington Wizards, and Verizon Center.

ORGANIZATION—Executives:

Mike Rizzo—General Manager and President of Baseball Operations.

- Born in Chicago in 1960, Rizzo was previously the Director of Scouting for the Arizona Diamondbacks beginning in 2000. Rizzo joined the Nats in 2007 as an assistant general manager.

- Succeeded Jim Bowden as the General Manager in 2009, and was promoted to team president in 2013.

- Drafted by the Angels in the 22nd round of the 1982 MLB Draft, and reached Class A Advanced with the Redwood Pioneers.

- Began his scouting career with the Chicago White Sox, and joined the Diamondbacks in their first year, 1998.

- His father, Phil Rizzo, is a special advisor to the GM of the Washington Nationals (Mike Rizzo, his son). Phil (born 1929) is a member of the inaugural class (2008) of the Professional Baseball Scouts Hall of Fame.

Bob Boone—Vice President of Player Personnel

- Born in San Diego in 1947, former catcher with the Phillies, Angels, and Royals (1972-90), and manager for the Royals (1995-97) and Reds (2001-03), he was a four time All-Star and seven time Gold Glove Award winner.

- Son of a major league player, the late third baseman Ray Boone, and the father of two major leaguers: former second baseman, Bret Boone, and former utility infielder, Aaron Boone. All four were All-Stars during their careers.

Kris Kline — Asst General Manager & Vice President, Scouting Operations

- Born in Oak Harbor, WA in 1961 played minor league baseball for the Angels (roomed with Mike Rizzo in 1983!) for four years, and then transitioned to scouting with the team for the next ten years.

- Has been with the Nats in scouting since October 2006. Before that he spent seven years scouting for the Arizona Diamondbacks, earning a World Series ring in 2001.

Bill Singer — Director of International Scouting

- Born in Los Angeles in 1944, former MLB pitcher ("Sing Sing" and "The Singer Throwing Machine") and had a fourteen year career, primarily with the Dodgers and Angels. He was a two time All-Star, and pitched a no-hitter on July 20, 1970 (Dodgers).

Mike Wallace — Clubhouse and Equipment Manager

- Born circa 1959, would qualify as one of the longest serving team members, having come over from the Expos when the Nats moved to D.C. in 2005. During the summer of 2005, he slept many nights at RFK (not the most comfy place, as we all remember).

- Has worked in MLB clubhouses for almost four decades, beginning with the Washington Senators when they became the Texas Ranges in Arlington, TX. His mother was in charge of laundry, and he made four dollars a day for putting out laundry, shining shoes, and running errands.

- Borrowed Gaylord Perry's Lincoln Continental for his junior prom! Graduated from the University of Texas Arlington in 1984 with a BS in PE/Health.

- "Wally" makes everything work for the team at home and on the road.

PITCHERS—
All-Time LEADERS—Single Season

ERA:	Starters: Doug Fister 2.41 (2014)
	Relievers: Drew Storen 1.12 (2014)
Wins:	Gio Gonzalez 21 (2012)
Strikeouts:	Max Scherzer 276 (2015)
Saves:	Chad Cordero 47 (2005)
WHIP:	Starter: Max Scherzer 0.92 (2015)
	Relievers: Joel Peralta 0.80 (2010)
Innings Pitched:	Livan Hernandez 246.1 (2005)
Quality Starts:	Jordan Zimmermann 24 with 0.75% in both 2012 and 2014
	Stephen Strasburg 24 with 0.71% in 2014
Complete Games:	Jordan Zimmermann 4 (2013),
	Max Scherzer 4 (2015)

Shutouts:	Max Scherzer 3 (2015)
No-Hitters:	Max Scherzer 2 (2015)
	Jordan Zimmermann 1 (2014)
Wild Pitches:	Henry Rodrigues 14 (2011)
Total Batters Faced:	Livan Hernandez 1065 (2005)
Balks:	Stephen Strasburg 3 (2013)
Save Opportunities:	Rafael Soriano 49 (2013)
Bases on Balls:	Livan Hernandez 84 (2005)
Losses:	Ramon Ortiz 16 (2006)
Home Runs Given Up:	Ramon Ortiz 31 (2006)
K/9:	Max Scherzer 10.863 (2015)
K/BB:	Max Scherzer 8.118 (2015)
KO%:	Max Scherzer 30.7 (2015)

PITCHERS—
Top 3 Leaders Per Category

(#1 HIGHLIGHTED)

COMPLETE GAMES—Top 3 Nats—Single Season

1. 4—Max Scherzer (2015)

2. 3—Jordan Zimmermann (2014)

3. 2—Gio Gonzalez (2012)

Fun Fact: Since 1945, Bob Feller (Indians) holds the record for complete games with 36 in 1946. In 2014, the leader was Clayton Kershaw (Dodgers) with 8 complete games.

GAMES FINISHED—Top 3 Nats—Single Season

1. 62—Chad Cordero (2005)

2. 59—Chad Cordero (2007)

3. 59—Chad Cordero (2006)

Fun Fact: In 2014, the leader for Games Finished was Francisco Rodriguez (Brewers) with 66

BAA - Batting Average Against (Starting Pitchers)

1. .206—Gio Gonzalez (2012)

2. .207—Stephen Strasburg (2013)

3. .208—Max Scherzer (2015)

Fun Fact: The single season record is held by Pedro Martinez (Red Sox) with .167 (2000, Boston).

RUNS GIVEN UP:

1. 127—Ramon Ortiz (2006)

2. #2: 116—Livan Hernandez (2005)

3. #3: 110—Tim Redding (2008)

HITS GIVEN UP:

1. #1: 268—Livan Hernandez (2005)

2. #2: 230—Ramon Ortiz (2006)

3. #3: 227—Esteban Loaiza (2005)

GO: GROUND OUTS—Pitcher Induced—Single Season

1. #1: 335—John Lannan (2009)

2. #2: 293—Livan Hernandez (2005)

3. #3: 285—John Lannan (2008)

Fun Fact: Roy Halladay (Blue Jays) holds the record for most ground outs with 422 in 2003.

GIDP: GROUNDED into DOUBLE PLAYS— Pitcher Induced—Single Season

1. #1: 28—John Lannan (2009)

2. #2: 26—John Lannan (2011)

3. #3: 25—Esteban Loaiza (2005)

Fun Fact: Scott Erickson (Orioles) holds the record for GIDP with 41 in 1999.

AO: FLY OUTS—Pitcher Induced—Single Season

1. #1: 288—Livan Hernandez (2005)

2. #2: 269—Livan Hernandez (2010)

3. #3: 261—John Patterson (2005)

Fun Fact: Ricky Helling (Rangers) holds the record for most fly outs with 336 in 2000.

HOME RUNS given up—Single Season

1. #1: Ramon Ortiz 31 (2006)

2. #2: Dan Haren 28 (2013)

3. #3: Tim Redding 27 (2008)

Fun Fact: In 2014, the MLB leader with the most HR's given up was Marco Estrada (Milwaukee) with 29.

WALKS given up—Single Season

1. #1: Livan Hernandez 84 (2005)

2. #2: Gio Gonzalez 76 (2013)

3. #3: Gio Gonzaliz 76 (2012)

Fun Fact: In 2014, the MLB leader with most walks was A.J. Burnett (Phillies) with 96.

LOSSES—Most Single Season

1. #1: Ramon Ortiz 16 (2006)

2. #2: John Lannan 15 (2008)

3. #3: Dan Haren 14 (2013)

Fun Fact: In 2014, the MLB leader with the most losses was A.J. Burnett (Phillies) with 18.

WILD PITCHES

1. #1: 14—Henry Rodriguez (2011)

2. #2: 10—Daniel Cabrera (2009)

3. #3: 10—Gio Gonzalez (2012)

Fun Fact: In 2014, the MLB leader with the most wild pitches was Garrett Richards (Angels) with 22.

BALKS

1. #1: 3—Yunesky Maya (2010)

2. #2: 3—Ramon Ortiz (2006)

3. #3: 3—Stephen Strasburg (2013)

Fun Fact: Dave Stewart holds the MLB single season record for balks with 16 in 1988.

TOTAL BATTERS FACED

1. #1: 1065—Livan Hernandez (2005)

2. #2: 912—Estaban Loaiza (2005)

3. #3: 899—Max Scherzer (2015)

Fun Fact: Since 1900, the leader in Total Batters Faced was "Iron" Joe McGinnity (Orioles) with 1,631 in 1901. Since WWII, Mickey Lolich (Tigers) faced 1,538 batters in 1971.

NUMBER OF PITCHES THROWN

1. #1: 4,012—Livan Hernandez (2005)

2. #2: 3,359—Max Scherzer (2015)

3. #3: 3,344—Estaban Loaiza (2005)

Fun Fact: In 2014, David Price (Tigers) was the leader for the most pitches thrown with 3,730 pitches.

HIT BATSMEN

1. #1: 18—Ramon Ortiz (2006)

2. #2: 18—Tony Armas (2006)

3. #3: 13—Livan Hernandez (2005)

Fun Fact: Since 2000, the leader in Hit Batsmen was Kerry Wood (Cubs) with 21 in 2003.

HOLDS (enters in save .1 IP and does not surrender the lead)

1. #1: 40—Clippard (2014)

2. #2: 38—Clippard (2011)

3. #3: 33—Clippard (2013)

Fun Fact: The most holds in a single season is 41 by Joel Peralta (Rays) in 2013.

NATS PITCHERS—

ALL-TIME CUMULATIVE TOTALS 2005-2015

Category	Statistic	Player
Wins	70	Jordan Zimmermann RHP
ERA	3.09	Stephen Strasburg RHP
Saves	95	Drew Storen RHP
Strikeouts	903	Jordan Zimmermann RHP
WHIP (walks & hits per innings pitched)	1.10	Stephen Strasburg RHP
BAA	.228	Stephen Strasburg RHP
IP	1094.0	Jordan Zimmermann RHP
Shutouts	4	Jordan Zimmermann RHP
Complete Games	8	Jordan Zimmermann RHP
Total Batters Faced	4218	Jordan Zimmermann RHP

HITTING—
BEST OF NATS PITCHERS—

NOTE: Only Nats Pitcher awarded a Silver Slugger Award: Stephen Strasburg in 2012

2005:	.244	Livan Hernandez (20 hits, 2 HR, 7 RBI, OPS .619)
2006:	.250	John Patterson #3 (.250, 2 hits)
	.267	Livan Hernandez #2 (12 hits, 6 RBI)
2009:	.214	Livan Hernandez (3 hits with 2/2B)
2010:	.200	Jordan Zimmermann (2 hits)
2011:	.217	Livan Hernandez (10 hits with 1/2B, 7 RBI)
	.209	Jordan Zimmermann (9 hits with 1/2B, 3 RBI)
2012:	.228	Edwin Jackson (13 hits)
	.277	Stephen Strasburg #1 (13 hits, 1 HR, 7 RBI, OPS .759)
2013:	.286	Tanner Roark (4 hits, 1 RBI, OPS .643)
2014:	.286	Craig Stammen (2 hits, 1 triple)
2015:	.226	Doug Fister (7 hits, 1 double, OPS .531)

Fun Fact: The pitcher with the most Silver Slugger Awards is Mike Hampton—with FIVE—from 1999-2003.

Possibly the most notable hitting pitcher in D.C. history (no Silver Slugger Award back then and before the AL DH!):

Walter Johnson: in 1925 with the SENATORS (36 games), he had one of the best single hitting seasons for a pitcher—at age 37. Johnson batted .433, had 2 HR's, 20 hits, scored 12 runs, and had an OPS of

1.033 (OBP .455 plus SLG .577). His CAREER averages over twenty-one years: .235 BA, 24 HR, .616 OPS.

THE PRESIDENTS

- **2005:** The opening season featured the PNC Dollar Derby: an animated cartoon depicting a car race between George Washington, Abraham Lincoln, and Alexander Hamilton.

- **2006:** The derby was replaced by the Presidents' Race, a cartoon with four presidents competing in a race through D.C.

- **July 21, 2006:** the live Presidents' Race was first held, featuring the four Mount Rushmore presidents: Washington, Roosevelt, Lincoln, and Jefferson (George, Teddy, Abe and Tom). They wore jerseys numbered according to their term as president (1 for George, 3 for Tom, 16 for Abe, 26 for Teddy).

- Teddy did not win for seven seasons, and a "Let Teddy Win" campaign started up.

- Teddy was known for using some desperate measures during his dry spell, including the use of zip lining, a golf cart, a rickshaw, and a motor scooter.

- **October 3, 2012:** Teddy finally won for the first time on October 3, 2012, during the first game played after the Nats reached the post season for the first time.

- **2013:** A new president, William Howard Taft (Bill) was added April 1, 2013. Bill has jersey number 27.

- **2015:** Calvin Coolidge became the sixth president to join the Nats team. Calvin's jersey is number 20.

PROMOTIONS—
Best Nats Promotions

Nats Stacking dolls—2015

Large to small: Scherzer Harper Zimmerman Cordero Frank Robinson

Okay, I was very excited about this one, which occurred on September 3, 2015. I was out of town, so my son went and got one for me! It is one of my favorites!

Jayson Werth GARDEN GNOME—2014

This was huge! And on a weekday! (Tuesday, August 5, 2014) I spent almost two hours getting to the game and then let my spouse out to run for the gate to make sure we got one. This was after missing out on the Jayson Werth Bobblebeard at the Potomac Nationals because of being too far back in line. Werth ended up having a bad night, unfortunately. On the other hand, attendance that night was 40,686—pretty good for a Tuesday!

"Take Back the Park" Campaign—2012

Selling single game tickets for the May 4 6, 2012 series against the Phillies that were available only to an address in D.C., VA, or MD. This was a welcome promotion after suffering all the Phillies fans filling Nationals Park. Fans responded and for those games attendance was enthusiastic: May 4th—34,377, May 5th—39,496, and May 6th—33,058!

First BOBBLEHEAD Giveaways:

- Chad Cordero: June 10, 2006
- Jose Guillen: July 7, 2006

JAYSON WERTH

Fun Fact: WORST Promotions in MLB History:

- Indians Ten Cent Beer Night: They were not so smart in the 70's! On June 4, 1974, the Cleveland Indians hosted this promotion and, due to the unruly behavior of the intoxicated crowd, the game had to be forfeited in the ninth inning to the visiting Texas Rangers (score was actually tied 5 5).

- Dodgers Baseball Give away Night: Another dumb idea, the Dodgers had a baseball give away promotion night on August 10, 1995. Needless to say, some of the 53,361 fans attending threw their free promotional baseballs on the field, resulting in a forfeit to the St. Louis Cardinals.

is for...

QUICK HOOK—
Notable Short Outings

NATS PITCHERS WITH THE FEWEST INNINGS (#1 HIGHLIGHTED)

0.1 innings	Yunesky Maya (2013)
0.2 innings	Tyler Moore (2015) an unexpected outing on the mound!
1.0 innings	Clint Robinson (2015) another hitter on the mound briefly…
1.0 innings	Ross Detwiler (2007)
1.0 innings	Chris Booker (2007)
2.0 innings	Victor Garate (2009)
2.1 innings	Antonio Osuna (2005)
2.1 innings	Jason Bergmann (2010)

QUOTES—NOTABLE QUOTES

"That's a clown question, Bro"—**Bryce Harper** (June 13, 2012) to a reporter who, instead of asking him about his second straight three hit game, inquired instead whether the nineteen year old was going to celebrate with a legal Canadian beer. (Reporter Chuck Schilken in the Los Angeles Times)

"For the Washington Senators, the worst time of the year is the baseball season." **(Roger Kahn)**

"First in war, first in peace, and last in the American League." (Senators)

"I tried to copy Earl Weaver. I think it was my first week of managing in New York and I came out to home plate, starting arguing with the umpire, kicking dire around. And they threw me out and said, 'We ain't taking Earl Weaver crap here.'" **Davey Johnson,** asked who he models his managerial style after. (Washington Post, James Wagner, October 2, 2014)

"Well none of my guys could, 'cause we can't score.'" **Davey Johnson,** reacting to the news that Boston's Mike Napoli apparently was dating a porn star. (Same as above)

"If I knew you were going to second guess me, I would have called back sooner." **Davey Johnson,** returning a reporter's phone call, on his decisions from NLDS Game 5 in 2012. (Same as above)

"World Series or bust. That's probably the slogan this year. But I'm comfortable with that." **Davey Johnson's** infamous line. (Same as above)

"You win games, I lose them." **Davey Johnson's** favorite line to his players. (Same as above)

QUALITY STARTS (QS %)—

(QS: Pitcher goes at least 6 innings and gives up 3 or less earned runs)

Year	QS	Pitcher
2005:	24	Esteban Loaiza RHP (71%)
2006:	15	Ramon Ortiz RHP (45%)
2007:	11	Shawn Hill RHP (54%)
2008:	21	John Lannan LHP (68%)
2009:	19	John Lannan LHP (58%)
2010:	22	Livan Hernandez RHP (67%) (TIED #3)
2011:	16	Jordan Zimmermann RHP (62%)
2012:	24	Jordan Zimmermann RHP (75%) (TIED #1)
	22	Gio Gonzalez LHP (69%) (TIED #3)
2013:	21	Jordan Zimmermann RHP (66%)
	21	Gio Gonazalez LHP (66%)
2014:	24	Jordan Zimmermann RHP (75%) (TIED #1)
	24	Stephen Strasburg RHP (71%) (TIED #1)
2015:	23	Max Scherzer RHP (79%) #2

Fun Fact: Since 1920, the most Quality Starts record is held by Wilbur Wood (White Sox) with 37 in 1971; Bob Feller and Sandy Koufax both had 36. The percentage leader in Quality Starts is Greg Maddux (Braves) with 24 out of 25 games in 1994 for 96%.

QUALITY STARTS—
Nats TEAM Ranking *(#1 team that year)*

2005	84	#12 in MLB (Astros #1 with 103)
2006	68	#25 in MLB (Angels #1 with 97
2007	60	#28 in MLB (Indians #1 with 94)
2008	67	#27 in MLB (Diamondbacks #1 with 95)
2009	63	#29 in MLB (Braves #1 with 99)
2010	69	#30 in MLB (Athletics #1 with 103)
2011	79	#24 in MLB (Phillies #1 with 108)
2012	97	#5 in MLB (Mets #1 with 101)
2013	91	#10 in MLB(Tigers #1 with 108)
2014	106	#2 in MLB (Braves #1 with 110)
2015	91	#8 in MLB (Cardinals #1 with 106)

is for...

*R*BI (Runs Batted in)—

Year	RBI	Player
2005	76	Jose Guillen
2006	110	Ryan Zimmerman (#1)
2007	91	Ryan Zimmerman
2008	61	Lastings Milledge
2009	106, 105	Ryan Zimmerman (#2, 106), Adam Dunn (#3, 105)
2010	103	Adam Dunn
2011	95	Michael Morse
2012	100	Adam LaRoche
2013	82	Jayson Werth
2014	92	Adam LaRoche
2015	99	Bryce Harper

Fun Fact: The MLB single season record holder for RBI is Hack Wilson (Cubs) with 191 in 1930. Second on the list is Lou Gehrig (Yankees) with 185 in 1931. Since 1945, Ted Williams (Red Sox) had 159 in 1949 and, more recently, Sammy Sosa (Cubs) had 158 in 1998. Alex Rodriguez (Yankees) had 156 in 2007. Hack Wilson's record of 191 is considered one of the records unlikely to be broken.

RUNS SCORED—

2005:	81	Jose Guillen
2006:	119	Alfonso Soriano (#1)
2007:	99	Ryan Zimmerman
2008:	77	Cristian Guzman
2009:	110	Ryan Zimmerman
2010:	85	Adam Dunn
2011:	73	Michael Morse
2012:	98	Bryce Harper
2013:	84	Jayson Werth
2014:	111	Anthony Rendon (#3)
2015:	118	Bryce Harper (#2)

Fun Fact: The MLB single season record holder (since 1900) is Babe Ruth OF (Yankees) with 177 in 1921. The NL Record is held by Rogers Hornsby 2B (Cubs) with 156 in 1929.

RAR—Runs Above Replacement

(number of runs this player is better than a replacement player) —

2005:	37.0	Jose Guillen RF
2006:	55.6	Alfonso Soriano LF
2007:	46.5	Ryan Zimmerman 3B
2008:	30.4	Willie Harris LF

2009:	66.0	Ryan Zimmerman 3B #2
2010:	63.9	Ryan Zimmerman 3B #3
2011:	30.9	Danny Espinosa 2B
2012:	44.5	Ian Desmond SS
2013:	44.7	Ian Desmond SS
2014:	59.5	Anthony Rendon 3B
2015:	89.4	Bryce Harper #1 (#1 in MLB)

Fun Fact: in 2015, Mike Trout OF (Angels) had the second highest RAR ranking with 84.9; Josh Donaldson (Blue Jays) was third with 82.4.

RAA and wRAA—Runs Better than Average (number of runs this player is better than a league average player) and Weighted Runs Above Average

LEADERS EACH SEASON (#1-2-3 HIGHLIGHTED) (RAA: BASEBALL REFERENCE.COM) (WRAA: FRANGRAPHS.COM)

Year	RAA	Player	wRAA	Player
2005	20	Nick Johnson 1B	26.9	Nick Johnson 1B
2006	42	Alfonso Soriano LF	38.9	Nick Johnson 1B (#2)
2007	26	Ryan Zimmerman 3B	18.6	Dmitri Young 1B
2008	29	Cristian Guzman SS	7.7	Cristian Guzman SS
2009	52	Ryan Zimmerman 3B (#2)	36.7	Adam Dunn 1B
2010	43	Ryan Zimmerman 3B	31.0	Adam Dunn 1B
2011	15	Michael Morse 1B	33.7	Michael Morse 1B
2012	31	Bryce Harper LF	23.8	Adam LaRoche 1B
2013	29	Jayson Werth RF	37.0	Jayson Werth RF
2014	44	Anthony Rendon 3B (#3)	32.2	Jayson Werth RF
2015	77	Bryce Harper RF (#1) (#1 MLB)	77.3	Bryce Harper RF (#1) (#1 MLB)

Fun Fact: The single season leader in wRAA is Babe Ruth OF (Yankees) with 127.9 in 1921. In 2015, Mike Trout OF (Angels) had the second highest RAA ranking with 66.

RELIEF PITCHING—SAVES

- **2005:** 47—Chad Cordero RHP (#1) (#1 in MLB)
- **2006:** 29—Chad Cordero RHP
- **2007:** 37—Chad Cordero RHP (#3)
- **2008:** 17—Jon Rauch RHP
- **2009:** 20—Mike MacDougal RHP
- **2010:** 26—Matt Capps RHP
- **2011:** 43—Drew Storen RHP (TIED #2)
- **2012:** 32—Tyler Clippard RHP
- **2013:** 43—Rafael Soriano RHP (TIED #2)
- **2014:** 32—Rafael Soriano RHP
- **2015:** 29—Drew Storen RHP

Fun Fact: The pitcher with the all-time most single season saves is Francisco Rodriguez RHP (Angels) with 62 in 2008 (out of 69 save opportunities). The most career saves record is held by Mariano Rivera RHP (Yankees) with 652.

RELIEF PITCHING—STRIKEOUTS (KO)

Year	KO	Player
2005	61	Chad Cordero RHP
2006	69	Chad Cordero RHP
2007	71	Jon Rauch RHP
2008	93	Joel Hanrahan RHP (#3)
2009	67	Tyler Clippard RHP
2010	112	Tyler Clippard RHP (#1)
2011	104	Tyler Clippard RHP (#2)
2012	87	Craig Stammen RHP
2013	79	Craig Stammen RHP
2014	82	Tyler Clippard RHP
2015	67	Drew Storen RHP

RING OF HONOR
at Nationals PARK

The Nats established the Ring of Honor in 2010 to celebrate HOF players with ties to D.C. baseball via the Washington Senators, the Homestead Grays, the Montreal Expos and the Washington Nationals. Their names are featured above the PNC Diamond Club behind home plate (19 names):

- James "Cool Papa" Bell—Homestead Grays CF (1932, 1943-46)

- Ray Brown—Homestead Grays P (1932-45, 1947-48)

- Gary Carter—Montreal Expos C (1974-84, 1992)

- Joe Cronin—Washington Senators SS (1928-34)

- Andre Dawson—Montreal Expos CF (1976-86)

- Rick Ferrell—Washington Senators C (1937-41, 1944-45, 1947)

- Josh Gibson—Homestead Grays C (1937-46)

- Goose Goslin—Washington Senators LF (1921-30, 1933, 1938)

- Clark Griffith—Washington Senators owner, player and manager (1912-55)

- Bucky Harris—Washington Senators manager/player (1919-28, 1935-42, 1950-54)

- Walter Johnson—Washington Senators P (1907-27)

- Harmon Killebrew—Washington Senators 1B (1954-60)

- Buck Leonard—Homestead Grays 1B (1934-50)

- Heinie Manush—Washington Senators LF (1930-35)

- Cumberland Posey—Homestead Grays manager, player, owner (1911-46)

- Sam Rice—Washington Senators RF (1915-33)

- Frank Robinson—Manager of the Nationals (2005-06)

- Jud Wilson—Homestead Grays 3B (1931-32, 1940-45)

- Early Wynn—Washington Senators P (1939-44, 1946-48)

STATCAST Inaugural Season 2015—

A Few Highlights:

- Ian Desmond SS ranked #1 among shortstops for his tracked throws to 1st base with an average of 82.5 mph.

- Michael Taylor CF had the 2nd longest home run of the regular season at 492.8 feet.

- Ian Desmond had the 11th longest home run at 477.1 feet.

- Bryce Harper is 17th on the exit velocity list with a launch speed of 116.0.

STADIUMS in D.C.

BOUNDARY FIELD/NATIONAL PARK 1891-1911

Predecessor to GRIFFITH Stadium on the same site, it was destroyed by fire in March 1911, and was home to the Washington Senators from 1903 to 1911.

GRIFFITH STADIUM 1911-1965

Built in 1911, it was renamed for Senators owner Clark Griffith in 1920, and was home to the Washington Senators from 1911 to 1960. The 1937 and 1956 All-Star Games were played there, and also World Series games in 1924, 1925, and 1933. Capacity seating was about 29,000. It was also home to the Negro League Homestead Grays during the forties, and the Washington Redskins from 1937-1960. It was demolished in 1965 and is now the site of the Howard University Hospital.

RFK STADIUM—Baseball 1962-71 (Senators) and 2005-07 (Nats)

Opened originally as District of Columbia Stadium, it was renamed in 1969 for U.S. Senator and presidential candidate Robert F. Kennedy, who was assassinated in June 1968. It was designed as a "multi-sport" stadium and served as the home of the Washington Senators 1962-1971, and the Washington Nationals 2005-2007. RFK hosted two MLB All-Star Games in 1962 and 1969. When the Nationals played there, it was the fourth oldest active stadium after Fenway Park, Wrigley Field, and Yankee Stadium. The Redskins played at RFK 1961-66, and it has been the home for the D.C. United MLS Soccer team since 1996. Seating capacity for baseball was around 45,000.

Nationals PARK 2008 to Present

Nats Park is the first major league stadium to be accredited as a Leadership in Energy and Environmental Design (LEED) Structure. Opened on March 30, 2008, it features panoramic views of the riverfront, Navy Yard, and D.C. landmark buildings and features some popular concessions like Ben's Chili Bowl and Shake Shack. Inspiration for the look of the building is taken from the East Wing of the National Art Gallery, by architect I.M. Pei, and it cost $611 million to build. Seating capacity is 41,888.

NATS SPRING TRAINING STADIUM—FLORIDA

SPACECOAST STADIUM—Spring Training—Viera, FL

Since 2005, the Nats have held their spring training at what was the EXPO's location from 2003 04, and was the original spring site for the Marlins from1994 2002. Seating capacity is 8,100. The Nats plan to move spring training to a new site in West Palm Beach, FL as of 2017, which they will share with the Houston Astros.

SLASH LINES in MLB:

AVG/OBP/SLG

Slash lines represent a player's key offensive statistics: batting average/on base percentage/slugging percentage. A good slash line is .3xx/.4xx/.5xx. In 2015, BRYCE HARPER had a killer slash line: .330/.460/.649! Here are some other notable examples from Nats history:

Year	Slash Line	Player
2005	.289/.408/.479	Nick Johnson
2006	.290/.428/.520	Nick Johnson
2006	.277/.351/.560	Alfonso Soriano
2007	.320/.378/.491	Dmitri Young
2009	.267/.398/.529	Adam Dunn
2010	.307/.388/.510	Ryan Zimmerman
2011	.318/.397/.532	Jayson Werth
2014	.302/.355/.416	Denard Span
2015	.330/.460/.649	Bryce Harper

Fun Facts: Some historic slash lines include Nap Lajoie 2B (Athletics) who had .426/.463/.643 in 1901. Rogers Hornsby 2B (Cardinals) had .424/.507/.696 in 1924. Ted Williams OF (Red Sox) achieved .406/.553/.735 in 1941.

STOLEN BASES —

LEADERS EACH SEASON (#1-2-3 HIGHLIGHTED)

2005:	8	Brad Wilkerson
2006:	41	Alfonso Soriano (#1)
2007:	24	Felipe Lopez
2008:	24	Lastings Milledge
2009:	24	Nyjer Morgan
2010:	34	Nyger Morgan (#2)
2011:	25	Ian Desmond
2012:	21	Ian Desmond
2013:	21	Ian Desmond
2014:	31	Denard Span (#3)
2015:	16	Michael Taylor

Fun Fact: The MLB (since 1900) record is held by Rickey Henderson with 130 (1982—Oakland Athletics); the NL record is held by Lou Brock with 118 (1974—St. Louis Cardinals).

STOLEN BASES—
CAUGHT STEALING (CS)—

LEADERS EACH SEASON (#1-2-3 HIGHLIGHTED)

2005:	10	Brad Wilkerson LF (TIED #2)
2006:	17	Alfonso Soriano LF (TIED #1)
2007:	9	Felipe Lopez C
2008:	9	Lastings Milledge LF (#3)
2009:	10	Elijah Dukes CF
2010:	17	Nyger Morgan CF (TIED #1)
2011:	10	Ian Desmond SS tied (#2)

2012:	6	Danny Espinosa 2B
2013:	6	Ian Desmond SS
2014:	7	Denard Span CF
2015:	5	Ian Desmond SS

Fun Fact: Rickey Henderson OF (Athletics), who holds the record for most stolen bases, also holds the record for most times caught stealing in a single season with 42 times in 1982.

SACRIFICE BUNTS—

LEADERS EACH SEASON (#1-2-3 HIGHLIGHTED)

Year	SAC Bunts	Player
2005	14, 13	Livan Hernandez RHP (14, #2), Jamey Carroll IF (13, #3)
2006	9	Livan Hernandez RHP
2007	9	Matt Chico LHP
2008	13	Tim Redding RHP
2009	11	Livan Hernandez RHP
2010	15	Nyger Morgan CF (TIED #1)
2011	15	Livan Hernandez RHP (TIED #1)
2012	9	Gio Gonzalez LHP
2013	10	Stephen Strasburg RHP
2014	11	Tanner Roark RHP
2015	10	Gio Gonzalez LHP

Fun Fact: Ray Chapman SS (Indians) holds the record for sacrifice bunts (single season) with 67 in 1917. A sad fact is that Chapman is the only MLB player to have been killed by a pitch; that occurred in 1920. Eddie Collins 2B (White Sox) has the career record with 512.

SACRIFICE FLIES—

2005:	9	Jose Guillen (TIED #2)
2006:	5	Jose Guillen and Royce Clayton
2007:	7	Brian Schneider
2008:	7	Lastings Milledge
2009:	9	Ryan Zimmerman (TIED #2)
2010:	7	Ian Desmond
2011:	5	Ian Desmond
2012:	9	Adam LaRoche (TIED #2)
2013:	5	Anthony Rendon
2014:	8	Adam LaRoche (#3)
2015:	10	Ryan Zimmerman (#1)

Fun Fact: Gil Hodges 1B (Brooklyn Dodgers) holds the record for most sacrifice flies in a season with 19 (1954—Brooklyn Dodgers); Andre Dawson OF (Expos) is second with 18 in 1983. Eddie Murray 1B (Orioles) holds the career record with 128.

SWITCH HITTERS—
Notable Nats Each Season

2005: Jose Vidro 2B, Cristian Guzman SS

2006: Jose Vidro 2B, Felipe Lopez SS

2007: Dmitri Young 1B, Felipe Lopez SS, Nook Logan CF, Cristian Guzman SS

2008: Felipe Lopez 2B, Cristian Guzman SS, Dmitri Young 1B, Emilio Bonifacio 2B

2009: Josh Bard C, Anderson Hernandez 2B, Cristian Guzman SS

2010: *Cristian Guzman 2B, Danny Espinosa 2B*

2011: *Danny Espinosa 2B*

2012: *Danny Espinosa 2B, Steve Lombardozzi UT*

2013: *Danny Espinosa 2B, Steve Lombardozzi UT*

2014: *Danny Espinosa 2B, Jose Lobaton C, Asdrubal Cabrera 2B*

2015: *Danny Espinosa 2B, Jose Lobaton C, Wilmer Difo IF*

Fun Fact: Notable switch hitters in history include Mickey Mantle CF (Yankees), Chipper Jones 3B (Braves), Ozzie Smith SS (Cardinals), Eddie Murray 1B (Orioles) and Pete Rose 1B (Reds).

is for...

TRIPLES—

Year	Triples	Player
2005	7	Brad Wilkerson
2006	3	Bernie Castro
2007	6	Cristian Guzman
2008	5	Emilio Bonifacio
2009	7	Cristian Guzman
2010	7	Nyjer Morgan
2011	5	Ian Desmond
2012	9	Bryce Harper (#2)
2013	11	Denard Span (#1)
2014	8	Denard Span (#3)
2015	2	Ian Desmond, Michael Taylor, Dan Uggla

Fun Fact: The MLB all-time single season record for triples is held by Chief Wilson OF (Pirates) with 36 in 1912. The career all-time leader is Sam Crawford OF (Tigers 1899 1916) with 309. Both of these are records that are considered unlikely to be broken, even though they were both set in the early 1900s.

TOTAL BASES—

2005:	264	Jose Guillen
2006:	362	Alfonso Soriano (#1)
2007:	299	Ryan Zimmerman
2008:	255	Cristian Guzman
2009:	320	Ryan Zimmerman (#3)
2010:	299	Adam Dunn
2011:	287	Michael Morse
2012:	291	Adam LaRoche
2013:	272	Ian Desmond
2014:	290	Anthony Rendon
2015:	338	Bryce Harper (#2)

Fun Fact: The single season leader for total bases is Babe Ruth OF/P (Yankees) with 457 in 1921. The career record holder is Hank Aaron RF/1B (Braves) with 6,856.

TEAM RECORDS—WHEN THE NATS RANKED #1

- 2005 Season Saves #1 NL—51

- 2012 Season Wins #1 MLB—98

- 2012 Season ERA #1 NL—3.33

- 2012 Season Batting Average Against (BAA) #1 NL—.237

- 2012 Season WHIP #1 NL—1.22

- 2013 Season WHIP #1 NL—1.16

- 2014 Team ERA #1 MLB—3.03

- 2014 Season Wins #1 NL—96

TENURE—

WHICH CURRENT NATS HAVE BEEN AROUND THE LONGEST?

MOST YEARS with the NATS/EXPOS Organization:
Ian Desmond—Drafted in 2004 by the EXPOS, so with the Nats since 2005 (debut not until September 10, 2009)

MOST YEARS playing with the Nats (MLB):

1. Ryan Zimmerman (debut September 1, 2005)

2. Jordan Zimmermann (debut April 20, 2009)

3. Craig Stammen (debut May 21, 2009)

4. Ian Desmond (debut September 10, 2009)

5. Drew Storen (debut May 17, 2010)

6. Wilson Ramos (traded to Nats July 29, 2010)

7. Danny Espinosa (debut September 1, 2010)

8. Jayson Werth (began 2011 season)

9. Gio Gonzalez (began 2012 season)

10. Bryce Harper (debut April 28, 2012)

11. Denard Span (began 2013 season)

12. Anthony Rendon (debut April 21, 2013)

TEAM PAYROLL—*NATS ANNUAL PAYROLL*—

RANK # MLB (TEAM WITH HIGHEST PAYROLL)

(ESTIMATED—baseball reference.com)

Year	Nats Payroll	Highest Payroll	Lowest Payroll
2005	$48,581,500 (#23)	Yankees $208,306,817	Tampa $29,679,067
2006	$63,143,000 (#21)	Yankees $194,663,079	Marlins $14,671,500
2007	$36,947,500 (#28)	Yankees $207,039,045	Tampa $24,123,500
2008	$54,961,000 (#26)	Yankees $212,286,789	Marlins $21,811,500
2009	$64,384,000 (#27)	Yankees $210,330,039	Marlins $40,029,000
2010	$67,701,000 (#22)	Yankees $210,722,389	Pirates $37,443,000
2011	$68,492,928 (#21)	Yankees $206,275,028	Royals $35,712,000
2012	$92,386,000 (#14)	Yankees $197,977,900	Astros $37,651,000
2013	$112,493,250 (#11)	Dodgers $254,161,000	Astros $14,672,300
2014	$137,235,080 (#6)	Yankees $258,118,959	Marlins $42,365,400
2015	$155,842,000 (#6)	Dodgers $230,339,500	Astros $62,912,500

TEAM STATS

BATTING AVERAGE: RANKING in MLB
(who was #1) (best NATS year highlighted)

2005—.252: #30 in MLB (Red Sox #1 with .281)
2006—.262: #24 in MLB (Twins #1 with .287)
2007—.256: #26 in MLB (Yankees #1 with .290)
2008—.251: #26 in MLB (Rangers #1 with .283)
2009—.258: #24 in MLB (Angels #1 with .285)
2010—.250: #20 in MLB (Rangers #1 with .276)
2011—.242: #27 in MLB (Rangers #1 with .283)
2012—.261: # 9 in MLB (Angels #1 with .274)
2013—.251: #17 in MLB (Tigers #1 with .283)
2014—.253: #12 in MLB (Tigers #1 with .277)
2015—.251: #16 in MLB (Tigers #1 with .270)

STOLEN BASES: RANKING in MLB
(who was #1) (highest NATS year highlighted)

2005—45: #28 in MLB (Angels #1 with 161)
2006—123: #7 in MLB (Angels #1 with 148)
2007—69: #23 in MLB (Mets #1 with 200)
2008—81: #17 in MLB (Rays #1 with 142)
2009—73: #23 in MLB (Rays #1 with 194)
2010—110: #9 in MLB (Rays #1 with 172)
2011—106: #16 in MLB (Padres #1 with 170)
2012—105: #14 in MLB (Brewers #1 with 158)
2013—88: #14 in MLB (Royals #1 with 153)
2014—101: #12 in MLB (Royals #1 with 153)
2015—57: #27 in MLB (Reds #1 with 134)

RUNS: RANKING in MLB
(who was #1) (year with most NATS RUNS highlighted)

2005 — *639: #30 in MLB (Red Sox #1 with 910)*
2006 — *746: #24 in MLB (Yankees #1 with 930)*
2007 — *673: #30 in MLB (Yankees #1 with 968)*
2008 — *641: #28 in MLB (Rangers #1 with 901)*
2009 — *710: #21 in MLB (Yankees #1 with 915)*
2010 — *655: #25 in MLB (Yankees #1 with 859)*
2011 — *624: #24 in MLB (Red Sox #1 with 875)*
2012 — *731: #10 in MLB (Rangers #1 with 808)*
2013 — *656: #15 in MLB (Red Sox #1 with 853)*
2014 — *686: #9 in MLB (Angels #1 with 773)*
2015 — *703: #10 in MLB (Blue Jays #1 with 891)*

HITS: RANKING in MLB
(who was #1) (year with most NATS HITS highlighted)

2005 — *1367: #30 in MLB (Red Sox #1 with 1579)*
2006 — *1437: #24 in MLB (Yankees #1 with 1608)*
2007 — *1415: #26 in MLB (Yankees #1 with 1656)*
2008 — *1376: #27 in MLB (Rangers #1 with 1619)*
2009 — *1416: #10 in MLB (Padres #1 with 1315)*
2010 — *1355: #25 in MLB (Rangers #1 with 1556)*
2011 — *1319: #28 in MLB (Red Sox #1 with 1600)*
2012 — *1468: #7 in MLB (Rockies #1 with 1526)*
2013 — *1365: #19 in MLB (Tigers #1 with 1625)*
2014 — *1403: #12 in MLB (Tigers #1 with 1557)*
2015 — *1363: #23 in MLB (Tigers #1 with 1515)*

STRIKEOUTS (Batting): RANKING in MLB
(who was #1) (year with most NATS KO's highlighted)

2005—*1090: #9 in MLB (Reds #1 with 1303)*
2006—*1156: #8 in MLB (Marlins #1 with 1249)*
2007—*1128: #12 in MLB (Marlins #1 with 1332)*
2008—*1095: #13 in MLB (Marlins #1 with 1371)*
2009—*1208: #8 in MLB (Diamondbacks #1 with 1298)*
2010—*1220: #6 in MLB (Diamondbacks #1 with 1529)*
2011—*1323: #1 in MLB*
2012—*1325: #4 in MLB (Athletics #1 with 1387)*
2013—*1192: #18 in MLB (Astros #1 with 1535)*
2014—*1304: #9 in MLB (Cubs #1 with 1477)*
2015—*1344: #3 in MLB (Cubs #1 with 1518)*

WALKS: RANKING in MLB
(who was #1) (year with most NATS WALKS highlighted)

2005—*491: #16 in MLB (Red Sox #1 with 653)*
2006—*594: #7 in MLB (Red Sox #1 with 672)*
2007—*524: #17 in MLB (Red Sox #1 with 689)*
2008—*534: #20 in MLB (Red Sox #1 with 646)*
2009—*617: #5 in MLB (Yankees #1 with 663)*
2010—*503: #19 in MLB (Rays #1 with 672)*
2011—*470: #22 in MLB (Yankees #1 with 627)*
2012—*479: #17 in MLB (Rays #1 with 571)*
2013—*464: #20 in MLB (Rays #1 with 589)*
2014—*517: #7 in MLB (Athletics #1 with 586)*
2015—*539: #5 in MLB (Blue Jays #1 with 570)*

SHUTOUTS: RANKING in MLB

(who was #1) (year with most NATS SHUTOUTS highlighted)

2005—9: #16 in MLB (Marlins #1 with 15)
2006—3: #30 in MLB (Tigers #1 with 16)
2007—6: #25 in MLB (Padres #1 with 20)
2008—8: #19 in MLB (Red Sox #1 with 16)
2009—3: #30 in MLB (Giants #1 with 18)
2010—5: #26 in MLB (Phillies #1 with 21)
2011—10: #16 in MLB (Phillies #1 with 21)
2012—9: #20 in MLB (Braves #1 with 16)
2013—13: #9 in MLB (Dodgers #1 with 22)
2014—19: #3 in MLB (Cardinals #1 with 23)
2015—13: #8 in MLB (Cubs #1 with 21)

COMPLETE GAMES: RANKING in MLB

(who was #1) (year with most NATS CGs highlighted)

2005—4: #21 in MLB (Cardinals #1 with 15)
2006—1: #30 in MLB (Indians #1 with 13)
2007—0: #29 in MLB (Blue Jays #1 with 11)
2008—2: #26 in MLB (Blue Jays #1 with 15)
2009—6: #9 in MLB (Giants #1 with 11)
2010—2: #26 in MLB (Phillies #1 with 14)
2011—3: #21 in MLB (Phillies #1 with 18)
2012—3: #19 in MLB (Reds tied #1 with Tigers with 9)
2013—6: #5 in MLB (Rays #1 with 9)
2014—5: #8 in MLB (Giants tied #1 with Cardinals with 8)
2015—4: #12 in MLB (Indians #1 with 11)

BATTING AVERAGE AGAINST (BAA): RANKING in MLB

(who was #1) (best NATS year highlighted) (fangraphs.com)

2005—*.257: #12 in MLB (Athletics #1 with .238)*
2006—*.267: #17 in MLB (Padres #1 with .245)*
2007—*.263: #14 in MLB (Cubs #1 with .241)*
2008—*.264: #20 in MLB (Cubs 1 with .238)*
2009—*.270: #28 in MLB (Dodgers #1 with .228)*
2010—*.260: #22 in MLB (Giants #1 with .231)*
2011—*.250: #15 in MLB (Giants #1 with .228)*
2012—*.232: #2 in MLB/#1 in NL (Rays #1 with .225)*
2013—*.245: #11 in MLB (Reds #1 with .232)*
2014—*.241: #10 in MLB (Mariners #1 with .227)*
2015—*.246: #12 in MLB (Cubs #1 with .230)*

WHIP (walks/hits per innings pitched): RANKING in MLB

(who was #1) (best NATS year highlighted) (fangraphs.com)

2005—*1.37: #16 in MLB (Indians #1 with 1.22)*
2006—*1.48: #26 in MLB (Padres #1 with 1.27)*
2007—*1.44: #22 in MLB (Padres #1 with 1.27)*
2008—*1.45: #23 in MLB (Blue Jays #1 with 1.24)*
2009—*1.52: #29 in MLB (Dodgers #1 with 1.25)*
2010—*1.38: #22 in MLB (Phillies #1 with 1.25)*
2011—*1.30: #12 in MLB (Phillies #1 with 1.17)*
2012—*1.22: #2 in MLB/#1 in NL (Rays #1 with 1.17)*
2013—*1.23: #4 in MLB (Reds #1 with 1.17)*
2014—*1.16: #2 in MLB/#1 in NL (Athletics #1 with 1.14)*
2015—*1.21: #6 in MLB (Cubs #1 with 1.15)*

ERA: RANKING in MLB

(who was #1) (best NATS year highlighted)

2005—*3.87: #9 in MLB (Cardinals #1 with 3.49)*
2006—*5.03: #28 in MLB (Tigers #1 with 3.84)*
2007—*4.58: #19 in MLB (Padres #1 with 3.70)*
2008—*4.66: #24 in MLB (Blue Jays #1 with 3.49)*
2009—*5.00: #28 in MLB (Dodgers #1 with 3.41)*
2010—*4.13: #19 in MLB (Giants #1 with 3.36)*
2011—*3.58: #7 in MLB (Phillies #1 with 3.02)*
2012—*3.33: #2 in MLB/#1 in NL (Rays #1 with 3.19)*
2013—*3.59: #8 in MLB (Braves #1 with 3.18)*
2014—*3.03: #1 in MLB*
2015—*3.62: #7 in MLB (Cardinals #1 with 2.94)*

is for...

UP AND COMING NATS—

TOP PROSPECTS 2015 (FROM MLB.COM—2015 PROSPECT WATCH— NATIONALS, AUGUST 21, 2015):

1. **Lucas Giolito**—RHP

2. **Trea Turner**—SS (played in 27 games 2015 with Nats/MLB—44 plate appearances)

3. **Reynaldo Lopez**—RHP

4. **Wilmer Difo**—SS/2B (played in 25 games 2015 with Nats/MLB—11 plate appearances)

5. **Erick Fedde**—RHP

6. **A.J. Cole**—RHP (played in 3 games 2015 with Nats/MLB—9.1 innings pitched)

7. **Victor Robles**—OF

8. **Jakson Reetz**—C

9. **Pedro Severino**—C

10. **Austin Voth**—RHP

UNIFORM BASICS:

- Colors: Scarlet, navy blue, white/gray

- Primary Home: White jersey with red curly "W" on front and side, white pants, and red curly "W" cap

- Primary Away: Gray jersey with "Washington" center chest, gray pants, and navy curly "W" cap

- Alternate 1: Red jersey with white curly "W" on front and side, white pants and red curly "W" cap

- Alternate 2: Navy jersey with stars and stripes and curly "W" on front and side, white pants, Navy stars and stripes curly "W" cap

Infamous "NATINALS" Jersey:

On April 17, 2009, the Nats sent Adam Dunn and Ryan Zimmerman onto the field wearing "Natinals" jerseys for three innings. Dunn's jersey was auctioned off on May 3, 2009 to raise money for the Nats Dream Foundation; it brought in the highest bid of the night: $8,000!

Fun Fact: This was not the only case of misspelled jerseys: OF Joe Carter wore a "Torotno" Blue Jays jersey for six innings in 1994. Pitcher Aaron Harang took the mound for the Reds in 2005 wearing a "Cncinnati" jersey. In 2003, IF Adam Riggs played for the Angels in an "Angees" jersey. Giants OF Eugenio Velez showed up in a "San Francicso" jersey in 2010.

Baseball uniforms in history—**Fun facts!**

Uniform numbers:

Numbers on uniforms were tried unsuccessfully first by the Cleveland Indians on June 26, 1916 (left sleeve), and then by the St. Louis Cardinals in 1923 (sleeves again) who gave it up after being ridiculed by fans and opponents. Later in 1929, both the Yankees and Indians decided to try again and open their seasons with numbers on the backs of their uniforms beginning on April 16th. Due to a Yankee rainout that day, the Indians ended up being first and the Yankees the next day on April 17th, 1929. By the mid-1930s, all MLB team were wearing numbers.

Teams were originally assigned numbers based on the line up. Babe Ruth batted third so was number #3, and Lou Gehrig after him was #4. There is no real system now, except players like to stick with favorite numbers (from college, etc.), if possible.

Fun facts on uniform numbers:

First 0: Al Oliver of the Texas Rangers in 1978
First 00: Bob Newsome of the Washington Senators in 1943

Uniform names:

Started by the Chicago White Sox (GM Bill Veeck's idea) in 1960 on road uniforms, and included both home and road in 1961. The first misspelling occurred that year as well on Ted Kluszewski (not surprising!) with a backwards z, and x for the second k.

UNUSUAL NATS FACTS:

- 18 Inning Game NLDS Game 2 versus the Giants (October 4, 2014): Both catchers (Nats Wilson Ramos and GIANTS Buster Posey) played all 18 innings. It was also the longest game in postseason history by time, lasting 6 hours and 23 minutes. Tanner Roark turned 28 during the game!

- Jayson Werth—Third Generation MLB: Werth is on the short list of MLB families with three generations of players: grandson of Ducky Schofield and nephew of Dick Schofield, both MLB infielders, and stepson of Dennis Werth, who played with the Royals and Yankees from 1979 through 1982. His mom, Kim Schofield Werth competed in the U.S. Olympic Trials (long jump and 100 meters) and his dad was a football (and baseball) star at Illinois State University.

- Barry Bonds HR #756 (breaking Hank Aaron's record of 755 HRs): Washington Nationals pitcher Mike Bacsik was the pitcher who delivered the 86 mph fastball to Bonds in San Francisco at 8:51 p.m. on August 7th, 2007. Brian Schneider was the Nats catcher.

- Randy Johnson 300th Win: This occurred at Nationals Park on June 4th, 2009; Jordan Zimmermann was the losing pitcher. The score was Giants 5, Nats 1. Johnson was the 24th pitcher to reach this milestone. Johnson joined Steve Carlton as the only pitchers to win No. 300 against the organization with whom they made their debut; Johnson made his MLB debut with the EXPOS.

- Bryce Harper Youth Baseball Buddies: Harper played on a youth baseball team in Las Vegas with Kris Bryant and Joey Gallo, both of whom made their MLB debuts in 2015. Harper debuted in on April 28, 2012.

- Former Nat Adam Dunn is tied for 3rd on the all-time GOLDEN SOMBRERO list: Dunn is in good company being tied with Jim Thome and Bo Jackson with 18 games where he struck out 4 times (4 times in a game is the Golden Sombrero). Ryan Howard is first (24) and Reggie Jackson second with 22.

- Former Nat OF Rick Ankiel (currently serving as Nats Life Skills Coordinator) ranks with Babe Ruth: is the only other player besides Babe Ruth to start at least 10 games as a pitcher and hit at least 50 big league home runs.

UNIQUE HAIR
(Head and Facial) STYLES:

- Bryce Harper "Bro Hawk" 2013: On parade at the All-Star Game Home Run Derby, the impressive spiked Mohawk was apparently held up by "Suavecito Pomade."

- Bryce Harper "Pompadour" 2015: Harper was displaying a more flowing pompadour do in 2015; he told reporters it takes him about 30 minutes to do his hair before a game.

- Jayson Werth Shoulder Length Cool Dude Hair and Beard (ongoing): Surprisingly, Harper mentioned that Werth uses "Murray's" pomade. Looks like a natural 'do to us; I would be surprised if he is using product on that, but maybe it enhances the natural wave effects. He is maybe better known for his beard, which inspired the Jayson Bobble Beard (ran out before I got one!) and a special beard mania day at the Potomac Nationals.

- Danny Espinosa Fu Manchu 2015: He apparently spent the offseason growing a huge beard and then trimmed down to a bushy Fu Manchu mustache, which he shaved off during spring training.

- Gio Gonazalez Beard 2015: Gio is supposedly the first MBL athlete with a "sponsored" beard, having a four month promotion deal with men's grooming tool manufacturer Wahl. Gio said that having a beard "brings out the beast inside."

- Stephen Strasburg Clean 2015: Strasburg went the opposite direction in 2015 and showed up clean shaven, without his traditional goatee. Very nice.

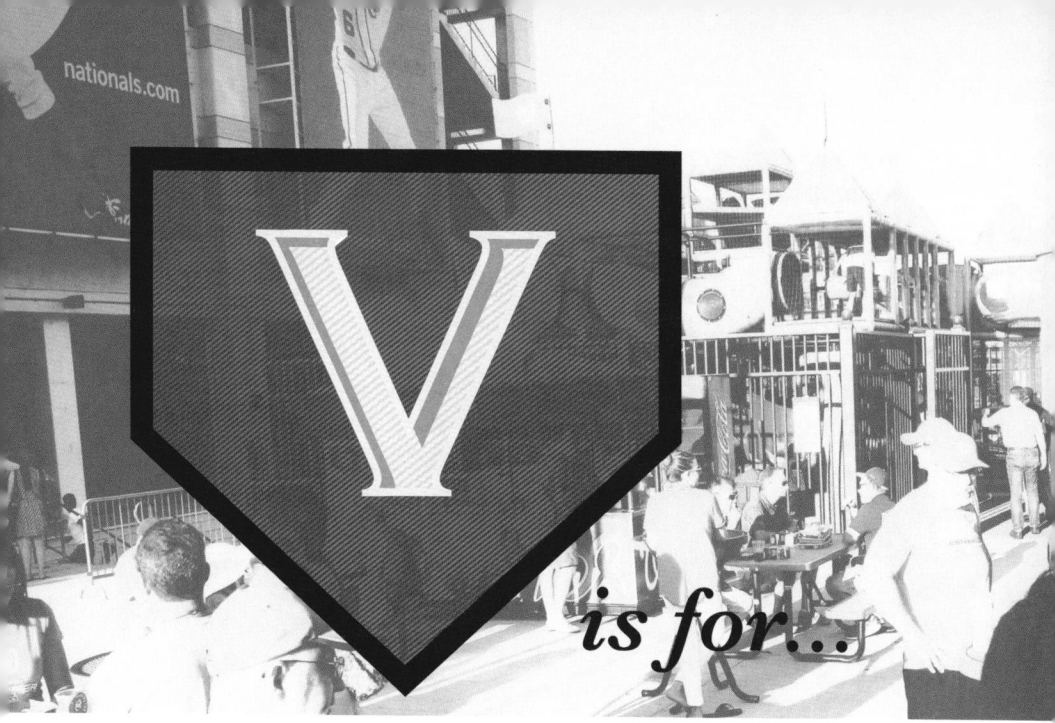

is for...

"**V**ALUE" Statistics

WAR (Wins Above Replacement)

(fangraphs.com)

What the Numbers Mean: 8+ is MVP level, 5+ is All-Star, 2+ Needs Improvement

Year	WAR	Player	MLB Leader
2005	3.7	Jose Guillen RF	Alex Rodriguez/Yankees (9.1)
2006	5.4	Alfonso Soriano LF	Albert Pujols/Cardinals (8.1)
2007	4.5	Ryan Zimmerman 3B	Alex Rodriguez/Yankees (9.6)
2008	3.0	Willie Harris LF	Albert Pujols/Cardinals (8.7)
2009	6.6	Ryan Zimmerman 3B (tied #2)	Ben Zobrist/Rays (8.6)
2010	6.6	Ryan Zimmerman 3B (tied #2)	Josh Hamilton/Rangers (8.4)

Year	WAR	Player	MLB Leader
2011	3.3	Danny Espinosa 2B	Jacoby Ellsbury/Red Sox (9.4)
2012	4.7	Ian Desmond SS	Mike Trout/Angels (10.3)
2013	4.8	Ian Desmond SS	Mike Trout/Angels (10.5)
2014	6.5	Anthony Rendon 3B (#3)	Mike Trout/Angels (8.0)
2015	9.5	Bryce Harper RF (#1)	BRYCE!

Fun Fact: The single season leader in WAR/Position Players is Babe Ruth (Yankee) with 14.1 in 1923. More recently, Carl Yastrzemski (Red Sox) had 12.4 in 1967 (his Triple Crown winning year).

WAR—Pitchers (Starters)

LEADERS EACH SEASON (#1-2-3 HIGHLIGHTED) (WHO WAS #1 IN MLB)

(fangraphs.com)

Year	WAR	Player	MLB Leader
2005	4.7	Esteban Loaiza RHP	Johan Santana/Twins (7.1)
2006	0.2	Ramon Ortiz RHP	Johan Santana/Twins (6.7)
2007	0.1	Matt Chico LHP	Jake Peavy/Padres (6.7)
2008	1.4	John Lannan LHP	Tim Lincecum/Giants (7.1)
2009	1.4	John Lannan LHP	Zack Greinke/Royals (8.6)
2010	2.9	Livan Hernandez RHP	Justin Verlander/Tigers (6.3)
2011	3.4	Jordan Zimmermann RHP	Roy Halladay/Phillies (8.3)
2012	5.0	Gio Gonazalez LHP (#3)	Justin Verlander/Tigers (6.8)
2013	3.7	Jordan Zimmermann RHP	Clayton Kershaw/Dodgers (7.19)
2014	5.3	Jordan Zimmermann RHP (#2)	Clayton Kershaw/Dodgers (7.7)
2015	6.4	Max Scherzer RHP (#1)	Clayton Kershaw/Dodgers (8.6)

Fun Fact: The single season record leader for WAR/Pitchers (since 1900) is Walter Johnson (Senators) with 14.6 in 1913. More recently, Steve Carlton (Phillies) had 12.0 in 1972.

VITAL STATISTICS

The tallest player in major league history is former Nationals pitcher Jon Rauch (2005-08) at 6'11". The tallest players on the list, including Randy Johnson at 6'10", are all pitchers. If you are wondering who the shortest player is, beside Eddie Gaedel (3'7") who played in one game as a promotion in 1951, the shortest player in the last thirty years would be current Houston Astro Jose Altuve at 5'5".

Tallest Nationals

Jon Rauch (RHP)	6'11"
Doug Fister (RHP)	6'8"
Daniel Cabrera (RHP)	6'7"
Matt Thornton (LHP)	6'6"
Dan Haren (RHP)	6'5"
Ross Detwiler (LHP)	6'5"
Jayson Werth (OF)	6'5"
Michael Morse (1B)	6'5"
Clint Robinson (1B/OF)	6'5"

Shortest Nationals

Matt Stairs (IF)	5'9"
Ivan Rodgriguez (C)	5'9"
Jhonatan Solano (C)	5'9"
Corey Patterson (OF)	5'9"
Nyger Morgan (CF)	5'10"

Notable Nationals on the Heavier Side

Dmitri Young (1B)	295 lbs.
Jon Rauch (RHP)	290 lbs.
Adam Dunn (1B)	285 lbs.
Austin Kearns (OF)	245 lbs.
Marlon Byrd (OF)	245 lbs.
Clint Robinson (1B/OF)	245 lbs.
Jayson Werth (OF)	240 lbs.

There are not many statistics on the "skinniest" players in MLB history; Eddie Gaedel (the shortest one time player mentioned above) would qualify here too at 65 pounds.

Notable Nationals on the Lighter Side:

Saul Rivera (P)	150 lbs.
Willy Taveras (OF)	160 lbs.
Damian Jackson (OF)	160 lbs.
Antonio Osuna (P)	160 lbs.
Jose Guillen (OF)	165 lbs.
Chris Snelling (OF)	165 lbs.
Trea Turner (SS)	175 lbs.

A future Nat in the making!

YOUNGEST/OLDEST NATS:

Youngest: **Bryce Harper OF**—*born October 16, 1992*
Oldest: **Matt Stairs UT**—*born February 27, 1968*

YOUNGEST/OLDEST NATS (by year):

Year	Youngest	Oldest
2005	Ryan Zimmerman 3B (20)	Mike Stanton LHP (38)
2006	Ryan Zimmerman 3B (21)	Mike Stanton LHP (39)
2007	Ross Detwiler LHP (21)	Dmitri Young 1B (33)
2008	Shairon Martis RHP (21)	Paul Lo Duca UT (36)
2009	Shairon Martis RHP (21)	Jamie Burke C (37)
2010	Stephen Strasburg RHP (21)	Ivan Rodriguez C (38)
2011	Stephen Strasburg RHP (22) Steve Lombardozzi 2B (22) Chris Marrero 1B (22)	Matt Stairs UT (43)
2012	Bryce Harper CF (19)	Mark DeRosa UT (37)
2013	Bryce Harper CF (20)	Jayson Werth RF (34)
2014	Bryce Harper CF (21)	Matt Thornton LHP (37)
2015	Pedro Severino RHP (21)	Matt Thornton LHP (38)

Fun Fact: In 1934, position player Charley O'Leary SS (Browns) came out of retirement to pinch hit for the Browns, becoming the oldest player to hit and score a run at age 58. Pitcher Satchel Paige was reportedly around 59 years old when he appeared in his last Major League game on September 25, 1965 for the Kansas City Athletics (a one-time appearance).

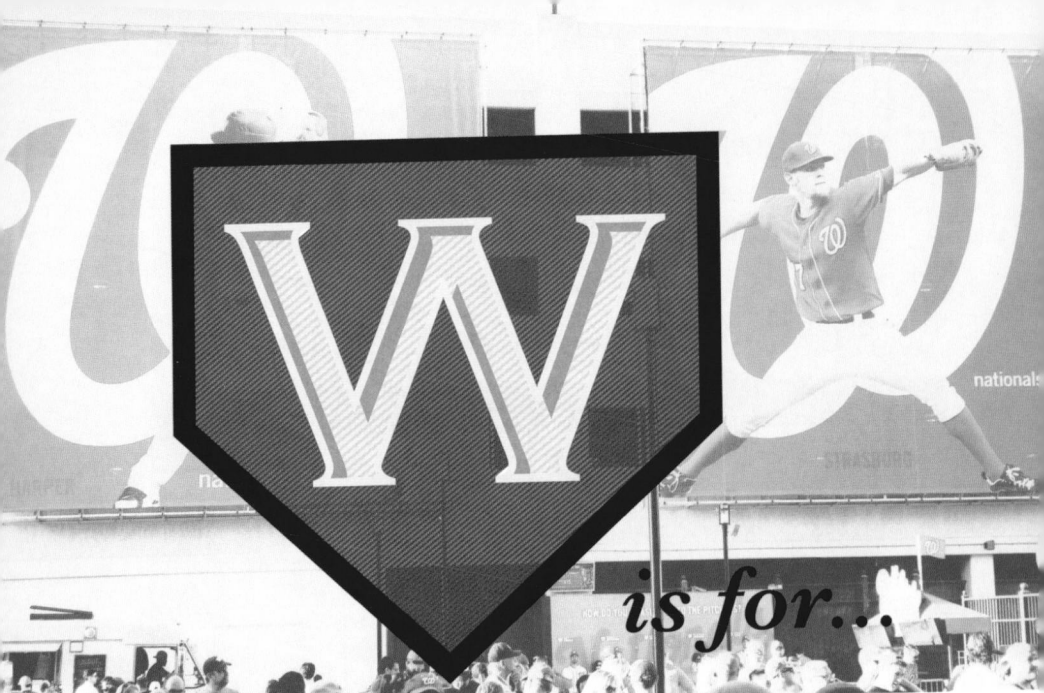

is for...

WINS—

Year	Wins	Player
2005	15	Livan Hernandez RHP
2006	11	Ramon Ortiz RHP
2007	8	Jon Rauch RHP
2008	10	Tim Redding RHP
2009	9	John Lannan LHP
2010	11	Tyler Clippard RHP
2011	10	John Lannan LHP
2012	21	Gio Gonzalez LHP (#1)
2013	19	Jordan Zimmermann RHP (#2)
2014	16	Doug Fister RHP (#3)
2015	14	Max Scherzer RHP

Fun Fact: Since 1900, the pitcher with the most wins is Jack Chesbro (R-NY Highlanders-AL) with 41 in 1904. The leading NL pitcher is Christy Mathewson (R-Giants) with 27 in 1908.

WPCT—Highest Win/Loss Percentage of NATS STARTING PITCHERS—

2005:	.600	Livan Hernandez RHP (15-10)
2006:	.529	Livan Hernandez RHP (9-8)
2007:	.500	Jason Bergmann RHP (6-6)
2008:	.476	Tim Redding RHP (10-11)
2009:	.625	Shairon Martis RHP (5-3)
2010:	.500	John Lannan LHP (8-8)
2011:	.615	Jason Marquis RHP (8-5)
2012:	.724	Gio Gonzalez LHP #2 (21-8)
2013:	.679	Jordan Zimmermann RHP #3 (19-9)
2014:	.737	Jordan Zimmermann RHP #1 (14-5)
2015:	.579	Gio Gonzalez LHP (11-7)

Note: Best Win/Loss Percentage in history belongs to Roy Face (Pirates) with .947 (18-1) in 1959. More recently, Cliff Lee (Indians) had .880 in 2008.

WHIP (walks plus hits per innings pitched)—

(mlb.com)

Year	WHIP Leader—Starter	WHIP Leader—Reliever
2005	John Patterson RHP (1.19)	Chad Cordero RHP (0.97)
2006	Mike O'Connor LHP (1.34)	Chad Cordero RHP (1.10)
2007	Jason Bergmann RHP (1.22)	Jon Rauch RHP (1.10)
2008	John Lannan LHP (1.34)	Jon Rauch RHP (1.01)
2009	Craig Stammen RHP (1.29)	Sean Burnett LHP (1.07)
2010	Livan Hernandez RHP (1.32)	Joel Peralta RHP (0.80)

Year	WHIP Leader—Starter	WHIP Leader—Reliever
2011	Jordan Zimmermann RHP (1.15)	Craig Stammen RHP (0.68)
2012	Gio Gonzalez LHP (1.13)	Christian Garcia RHP (0.79)
2013	Stephen Strasburg RHP (1.05, #2)	Tyler Clippard RHP (0.86)
2014	Jordan Zimmermann RHP (1.07, #3)	Drew Storen RHP (0.98)
2015	Max Scherzer RHP (0.92, #1)	Felipe Rivero LHP (0.95)

Fun Fact: The all-time leader for Single Season WHIP is Pedro Martinez (Red Sox) with 0.7373 in 2000.

CURLY "W" Evolution:

- First adopted by the Washington Senators in 1963 and used until 1971 when the team moved to Texas.

- The previous Senators logo was the straight up "W".

- First years of Nats featured a logo that spelled out Washington Nationals over a baseball with stars underneath. Alternate logos featured the interlocking "D.C." Jerseys featured "Nationals" and Washington.

- In 2011, the Nats changed to jerseys and caps that prominently featured the curly "W" logo.

- According to Wikipedia, the Nats acquired the rights to the curly "W" from the Texas Rangers (where the Senators moved), though the Rangers still own the rights to the Senators name.

WHATEVER HAPPENED TO...?

Brad Wilkerson (CF):

National in 2005 (Expos 2001-04); lead-off hitter with the first ever hit in Nats history, the first grand slam and first hit for the cycle.

Traded to the Texas Rangers in December 2005 where he spent two years, then signed contracts with the Seattle Mariners and Toronto Blue Jays in 2008, and retired in 2009.

In July 2014, named head coach for the The King's Academy Lions, a middle school team in West Palm Beach, Florida.

Also coaches for USA Baseball, and was named Volunteer Coach of the Year by USA Baseball in 2014.

Nick Johnson (1B):

National from 2005-2009 (missing the 2007 season due to injury); longest remaining player on the Nats roster of players who relocated from the EXPOS

Traded to the Marlins, and then the Yankees in 2009

More injury problems, signed to minor league contracts by Cleveland in 2011 (played AAA with the Columbus Clippers), and Orioles in 2012

Earned major league spot with the Orioles but suffered a wrist injury on June 27, 2012, and did not play again

Retired from MLB on January 28, 2013 at age 34

Cristian Guzman (SS):

National from 2005-2010 (missing the 2006 season due to injury); got the first hit ever in the new Nationals Park on March 30, 2008:

Traded to the Texas Rangers on July 31, 2010

Received spring training invitations from two teams in 2011 but missed much of the season due to personal issues.

Per Wikipedia, now resides in New Jersey with his three children (Cristian Jr., Cris Anthony, Crisangelie), and wife Maria.

Livan Hernandez (SP):

National from 2005-06 and 2009-11; started and won first even Nats home game on April 14, 2005:

After leaving the Nationals, Hernandez played for the Atlanta Braves and Milwaukee Brewers in 2012

Spring training instructor and batting practice pitcher in 2014

Retired officially as a player on March 13, 2014

On May 4th of the 2015 season, the Nationals scheduled a promotion: Great Moments in Nationals History: Inaugural Game – Livan Hernandez Bobble Head

Brian Schneider (C):

Nationals catcher 2005-07 (Expos 2000-05), caught the first pitch from President George Bush at the Nationals first game at RFK in 2005:

Traded to the Mets November 30, 2007, along with Ryan Church, for Lastings Milledge. Played for the Philadelphia Phillies in 2010, and retired after the 2012 season.

Since 2014, manager of the Miami Marlins Advanced A affiliate, the Hammerheads; he had 50 wins in 2014. Schneider played for the Hammerheads in 1998 when they were an EXPOS affiliate. The Hammerheads play at Roger Dean Stadium, spring training home of the Miami Marlins and St. Louis Cardinals.

Chad Cordero (P):

With the Nationals 2005-08 (Expos 2003-05), the second youngest player to reach 100 saves:

Missed most of the 2008 season due to injury and was sent down to AAA Syracuse. He rejected the assignment and became a free agent, signing a minor league contracts with the Mariners (2009), the Mets (2010) and the Los Angeles Angels (2013).

In 2010, Cordero threw out the first pitch for the Nationals 2010 season.

Adam Dunn (1B, LF):

National from 2009-10; hit 3 home runs in one game on July 7, 2010:

Traded to the White Sox in December 2010, and then to the Athletics on August 31, 2014.

Reached the postseason when the A's clinched the second AL Wild Card spot. Dunn did not get to play, however, and retired after the game.

At the time of his retirement, Dunn was tied for most opening day home runs at 8 with Frank Robinson and Ken Griffey, Jr.,

In 2013, appeared in the film "Dallas Buyers Club" as a bartender (he was also an investor in the film).

Jose Guillen (RF):

National 2005-06; team leader that year for RBI (76), runs (81), and hits (156).

Signed with the Mariners for the 2007 season, went on to play for the Royals (2008-2010)

Traded to the Giants August 13, 2010; shortly after, he was placed on their restricted list for postseason eligibility because he was being investigated for the use of performance enhancing drugs.

John Patterson (RHP):

A National from 2005-07 (Expo 2004-05), pitched Nats first ever complete game shutout against the Dodgers on August 4, 2005.

Injuries plagued Patterson in 2006 and 2007, and he was released on March 2008.

Signed a minor league contract with the Texas Rangers but was released on May 24, 2008.

According to Wikipedia, he lives in his hometown of Orange, Texas and got married in November 2007 to Shannon Schambeau, 2005 Miss District of Columbia and 4th runner up in the Miss America pageant.

Austin Kearns (OF):

With the Nationals from 2006-09; on May 12, 2007 at a home game, he hit a bases empty inside the park home run, the first ever for a Nationals player.

Became a free agent in November 2009, signed a minor league contract with the Cleveland Indians and was added to their Major League roster.

Traded to the New York Yankees (2010), back to the Indians (2011) and the Miami Marlins (2012).

In June 2015, Kearns joined the Lexington (KY) Christian Academy (LCA) baseball coaching staff as a volunteer assistant.

John Lannan (LHP):

With the Nationals from 2007 to 2012, making his MLB debut on July 26, 2007; Lannan was ejected in the fifth inning of that first MLB outing after hitting Chase Utley and then Ryan Howard.

Became a free agent after 2012 season, signed with the Phillies, but struggled with a 5.33 ERA in 74.1 innings.

Signed with the Rockies on a minor league contract in November 2014, and spent 2015 pitching for the Rockies Triple A Albuquerque Isotopes. He post a 3.97 ERA over 95.1 innings, and at thirty-one years old is hoping to move back up to the majors.

is for...

*X*BH (Extra Base Hits)—

(mlb.com)

2005:	60	Brad Wilkerson
2006:	89	Alfonso Soriano (#1)
2007:	72	Ryan Zimmerman
2008:	49	Cristian Guzman
2009:	73	Ryan Zimmerman (#3)
2010:	76	Adam Dunn
2011:	67	Michael Morse
2012:	69	Adam LaRoche
2013:	61	Ian Desmond
2014:	66	Anthony Rendon
2015:	81	Bryce Harper (#2) (#2 in NL)

Fun Fact: The single season record holder for XBH is Babe Ruth OF (Yankee) with 119 in 1921; Lou Gehrig 1B (Yankee) is second with 117 in

1927. Hank Aaron RF (Braves) has the career record with 1,477; Barry Bonds LF (Giants) is second with 1,440.

XBH%—STARTING PITCHERS
Extra Base Hit % (100+innings):

% of plate appearances ending with an EXTRA BASE HIT—

(baseball reference.com)

Year	XBH%	Player	League Average
2005	6.5	John Patterson RHP	8.0
2006	8.1	Mike O'Connor LHP	8.3
2007	9.1	Matt Chico LHP	8.1
2008	6.8	John Lannan LHP	7.9
2009	8.6	John Lannan LHP	7.8
2010	7.1	Livan Hernandez RHP	7.5
2011	6.4	John Lannan LHP	7.3
2012	5.7	Gio Gonzalez LHP (#2)	7.6
2013	4.5	Stephen Strasburg RHP (#1)	7.2
2014	6.0	Doug Fister RHP (#3)	7.1
2015	6.1	Jordan Zimmermann RHP	7.6

Fun Fact: In 2014, the two Cy Young winners had the following XBH%: Clayton Kershaw (NL/Dodgers) registered 5.7%, and Corey Kluber (AL/Indians) 6.9%.

X is for EXPOS—a little history about the Nationals franchise forerunner

- What's an EXPO? The team was named in honor of the 1967 world's fair, Montreal Expo 67. Another name under consideration at the time was the Voyageurs.

- 1981 NL East Champions

- HOF: Gary Carter (C) was the first HOF inductee depicted with an Expos cap on his plaque; Andre Dawson was the second inducted as an Expo. Other HOF inductees who played for the Expos during their careers: Randy Johnson, Pedro Martinez, and Tony Perez. Former managers Frank Robinson and Dick Williams are also HOF members.

- Retired EXPO Numbers: Gary Carter (8), Andre Dawson (10), Rusty Staub (10), Rim Raines (30), Jackie Robinson (42).

- Last EXPO Home Run—Brad Wilkerson on October 2, 2004 in the Expos' last win before becoming the Nationals, over the New York Mets 6-3

- Last Run Scored—Jamey Carroll on October 03, 2004

- The last remaining 2004 Expos on the Nationals roster to relocate with the team from Montreal: Nick Johnson (continuous—traded to the Marlins 2009) and Livan Hernandez (2003-06 and 2009-11).

- The other "last" Expo: Ian Desmond—drafted by the Expos in 2004 and a National as of 2015....though he did not make his MLB debut until September 10, 2009 for the Nats.

- About 27 Expos made the move to the Washington Nationals, including Jon Rauch, Luis Ayala, Gary Majewski, and Ryan Church, plus manager Frank Robinson and pitching coach Randy St. Claire.

- Record in 2004: 67-95, last place National League East. The Expos' opening day starting line up in 2004—compared to Nationals opening day line up 2005 (Wash.nationals.mlb.com):

2004 EXPOS	2005 NATS
1. Peter Bergeron CF	1. Brad Wilkerson CF
2. Jose Vidro 2B	2. Cristian Guzman SS
3. Carl Everett RF	3. Jose Vidro 2B
4. Orlando Cabrera SS	4. Jose Guillen
5. Brad Wilkerson 1B	5. Nick Johnson 1B
6. Tony Batista 3B	6. Vinny Castilla 3B
7. Termel Sledge LF	7. Termel Sledge
8. Brian Schneider C	8. Brian Schneider C
9. Livan Hernandez RHP	9. Livan Hernandez RHP

XRAYS—NOTABLE NATS INJURIES AND SURGERIES OVER THE YEARS

Nick Johnson—broken leg (fractured right femur) in a collision with teammate Austin Kearns on September 23, 2006. He missed the entire 2007 season.

Cristian Guzman—missed the 2006 season with a shoulder injury/surgery, returned in 2007.

Stephen Strasburg—Tommy John surgery in 2010 just several months into his major league career, rejoined the Nats on September 6, 2011.

Jayson Werth—broken wrist while attempting a sliding catch in May 2012; missed 3 months. Had a fractured wrist again when he got hit by a pitch on May 15, 2015. He returned in August 2015.

Bryce Harper—collided with the right outfield wall (face first) at Dodger Stadium on May 13, 2013. He received 11 stitches under his chin but did not suffer a concussion. He also bruised his neck and knee.

"YOU'RE OUTTA HERE":
Ejections and Umpires

Nats Manager with Most Ejections:
Jim Riggleman—11 ejections (Davey Johnson second with 4)

Fun Fact: Bobby Cox, former manager for the Atlanta Braves, holds the all-time record for ejections in MLB with 158; the record for most ejections in a single season is held by the legendary Giants manager John McGraw, with 13 in 1905.

Most EJECTIONS by Nats Player:
Bryce Harper—6 ejections (through 2015)

Most Ejections by an MLB Umpire:
Marvin Hudson—holds the record—ejected 9 Nats (2008-2015): Three in one game in 2010, 1 in 2012 and another three in one game

in 2013, and two in 2015 (see who and dates below). During that period, Hudson had a total of 25 ejections.

Fun Fact: Between 1990 and 2014, umpire Bob Davidson held the record for most ejections with 124 in 2,634 games (4.7%). Since 2005, the umpire with the most ejections in one year is Marty Foster with 14 in 2005; he and Joe West tied for the highest total of ejections 2005 through 2014 with 53.

The most famous Nats game in which the other team's player was ejected:

- On June 15, 2005 in a game versus the Angels in Anaheim, manager Frank Robinson asked the umpires to examine Angels reliever Brendan Donnelly's glove in the seventh inning, delaying the game for about 10 minutes. Angels manager Mike Scioscia confronted Robinson, and both benches emptied; though there were no punches thrown, Nats players had to restrain Jose Guillen, former Angel who was suspended by them late in the 2004 season for throwing a temper tantrum (this was his first visit back). Donnelly was ejected for having a foreign substance on his glove. To make things "interesting," Scioscia asked the umpires to examine Nats pitcher Gary Majewski's glove, which they did—and made him fix the loose laces on the glove.

- Guillen hit the home run that sparked an emotional Nats victory over the Angels, 6 3. Donnelly was suspended 10 days by MLB for having pine tar on his glove during the game (he never threw a pitch). Angels manager Scioscia and Nats manager Robinson were each suspended for one game and fined.

First Nats ejection:
- Earliest we could find was Marlon Byrd (Nats OF) on June 4, 2005, for arguing a strikeout, and then afterward he knocked down an umpire (Joe Brinkman) who stepped in the way between Byrd and the ejecting umpire. Byrd's suspension for the knockdown was overturned by MLB, who deemed that it was unintentional.

Nats coaches ejected (2008 through 2014):

Rick Eckstein —Batting Coach: 2 times (1-2009, 1-2010)

Dan Radison —1B Coach: 2 times (both in 2010)

Randy Knorr —Bench Coach: 1 time (2013)

Pat Corrales —Bench Coach: 1 time (2011)

Steve McCatty —Pitching Coach: 1 time (2015)

Lannan ejected in MLB debut: Nats pitcher John Lannan was ejected in his first MLB game on July 26, 2007 versus the Phillies. Lannan hit Chase Utley and then Ryan Howard on the next pitch, causing umpire Hunter Wendelstedt to immediately eject Lannan from the game. Nats beat the Phillies 7-6.

Fun Fact: Johnny Evers holds the career record for players (1902-29) with 50 ejections. HOF umpire Bill Klem holds the record for most career ejections (256 between1905 and1941) of active umpires. Bob Davidson has the most (156 between 1982 and present).

YOU'RE OUT!—UMPIRES AND EJECTIONS—2008 through 2015

(Beyondtheboxscore.com and portal.closecallsports.com)

NATS EJECTIONS—

UMPIRE (POS)—NUMBER EJECTED/DATE—EJECTED PLAYER/MANAGER:

2015:

- Rob Drake (home plate)—2 ejected/May 13 *(Bryce Harper RF, Mgr Matt Williams)*

- Marvin Hudson (home plate)—2 ejected/May 20 *(Bryce Harper RF, Mgr Matt Williams)*

- Andy Fletcher (home plate)—1 ejected/May 30 *(Yunel Escobar 3B)*

- Jerry Meals (home plate)—1 ejected/July 31 *(Bryce Harper RF)*

- Cory Blaser (home plate)—1 ejected/August 15 *(Steve McCatty, Pitching Coach)*

- Mark Repperger (home plate)—1 ejected/September 23 *(Jonathan Papelbon P)*

2014:

- Mark Wegner (Home plate)—1 ejected/June 23 *(Mgr Matt Williams)*

- Vic Carpazza (Home plate)—2 ejected/October 4 *(Mgr Matt Williams, Asdrubal Cabrera 2B)*

2013:

- John Hirschbeck (3B)—1 ejected/May 5 *(Bryce Harper LF)*

- John Trumpane (Home plate)—1 ejected/May 12 *(Kurt Suzuki C)*

- Hunter Wendelstedt (Home plate)—1 ejected/July 13 *(Bryce Harper LF)*

- Chad Fairchild (Home Plate)—1 ejected/July 20 *(Jayson Werth RF)*

- Mike Winters (Home plate)—1 ejected/July 25 *(Mgr Davey Johnson)*

- Marvin Hudson (Home plate)—3 ejected/August 17 *(Scott Hairston RF, Stephen Strasburg P, Mgr Davey Johnson)*

- Bill Welke (Home Plate)—1 ejected/September 19 *(Bench Coach Randy Knorr)*

2012:

- CB Bucknor (1B)—1 ejected/August 29 *(Bryce Harper LF)*

- Jerry Layne (Home plate)—1 ejected/September 6 *(Michael Gonzalez P)*

- Todd Tichenor (Home Plate)—1 ejected/September 8 *(Gio Gonzalez P)*

- Marvin Hudson (1B) — 1 ejected/September 15 *(Mgr Davey Johnson)*

2011:

- Tim Tschida (Home plate) — 1 ejected/April 6 *(Todd Coffey P)*
- Alfonso Marquez (Home plate) — 1 ejected/May 4 *(Mgr Jim Riggleman)*
- Todd Tichenor (Home plate) — 1 ejected/May 22 *(Mgr Jim Riggleman)*
- Ed Hickox (Home plate) — 1 ejected/May 27 *(Jerry Hairston 3B)*
- Rob Drake (Home plate) — 2 ejected/June 5 *(Jason Marquis P, Mgr Jim Riggleman)*
- Jeff Nelson (Home Plate) — 1 ejected/June 24 *(Jerry Hairston LF)*
- Mike Eastbrook (1B) — 1 ejected/June 24 *(Mgr John McLaren)*
- Joe West (3B) — 1 ejected/August 28 *(Mgr Davey Johnson)*
- Sam Holbrook (Home plate) — 1 ejected/August 28 *(Bench Coach Pat Corrales)*

2010:

- Paul Schrieber (Home Plate) — 1 ejected/April 12 *(Mgr Jim Riggleman)*
- Andy Fletcher (3B) — 1 ejected/April 16 *(Adam Dunn 1B)*
- Gerry Davis (Home plate) — 1 ejected/May 17 *(Batting Coach Rick Eckstein)*
- Mike Winters (1B) — 1 ejected/May 22 *(1B Coach Dan Radison)*
- Joe West (1B) — 1 ejected/June 4 *(Ian Desmond SS)*
- Dan Bellino (3B) — 1 ejected/June 5 *(Mgr Jim Riggleman)*
- Joe West (Home plate) — 1 ejected/June 5 *(Miquel Batista P)*

- Sam Holbrook (Home plate)—1 ejected/June 19 *(Mgr Jim Riggleman)*

- Sam Holbrook (Home plate)—1 ejected/August 17 *(Ivan Rodriguez C)*

- Scott Barry (Home Plate)—2 ejected/August 18 *(Ryan Zimmerman 3B, Mgr Jim Riggleman)*

- Rob Drake (1B)—2 ejected/August 28 *(1B Coach Dan Radison, Scott Olsen P)*

- Marvin Hudson (Home Plate)—3 ejected/September 1 *(Nyger Morgan CF, Doug Slaten P, Mgr Jim Riggleman)*

- Gary Cederstrom (Home Plate)—1 ejected/September 28 *(Mgr Jim Riggleman)*

2009:

- Tim Timmons (Home Plate)—1 ejected/April 17 *(Mgr Manny Acta)*

- Joe West (Home Plate)—1 ejected/July 30 *(Mgr Jim Riggleman)*

- Larry Vanover (3B)—1 ejected/August 11 *(Batting Coach Rick Eckstein)*

- Mike Reilly (Home Plate)—1 ejected/August 22 *(Mgr Jim Riggleman)*

2008:

- Angel Hernandez (Home Plate)—1 ejected July 8 *(Odalis Perez P)*

- Tim McClelland (Home Plate)—1 ejected May 17 *(Jesus Flores C)*

ZEROES—JORDAN ZIMMERMANN NO-HITTER and THE GREAT CATCH

Sunday, September 28, 2014 at 1:36 p.m.—game time: 2:01

- Nationals vs MARLINS: Game 162—last game of regular season

- 35,085 in attendance

- Ryan Zimmerman's 30th Birthday

- Denard Span set new team record for hits in a season

- 104 pitches—struck out 10, 79 strikes, walked 1

- First no-hitter by D.C. pitcher since Bobby Burke (Senators) on August 8, 1931.

- **Score:** Nats 1, MARLINS 0

- **WP:** Jordan Zimmermann (14-5) ERA 2.66

- **LP:** Henderson Alvarez (12-7) ERA 2.65

- **Hits:** Nats 11, Marlins 0

- **NATS SCORING:** Bottom of the 2nd—Ian Desmond solo HR

The Great Catch—Steven Souza Jr. saves Jordan Zimmermann's no-hitter

- ***9th inning:*** rookie late season call up Steven Souza Jr. went in to play LF, replacing Ryan Zimmerman. Adeiny Hechavarria grounded out to Jeff Kobernus at second (one out). Pinch hitter Jarrod Saltalamachia hit a deep fly to center caught by Michael Taylor (two outs). Marlin Christian Yelich is up with one more out to go…on a 2 1, 94 mile per hour fastball, belt high and right over the plate, smacks a horrifying "looks like a double" hit to the gap in left center.

- Souza turned, sprinted, and dove to make the sensational catch. "The one thing on my mind is, no matter how I'm going to get there, I'm going to get there," Souza said. "Getting there, I kind of blacked out."

- Souza held up his glove with the ball inside; Jordan Zimmermann raised up both arms, and the crowd of 35,085 did the same. Zimmermann could not believe it. "Whatever he wants he can have," Zimmermann said. "I'll buy him anything."

- "If somebody wrote that as an ending to the season," Storen said, "I don't think anybody would believe it."

- Souza's parents were there at the game to witness their son's amazing moment. Before the game, there was a ceremony recognizing Souza as the Nats minor league player of the year.

- Souza was born in Everett, Washington on April 24, 1989, and was drafted by the Nats in the third round of the 2007 MLB draft. In 2014, his performance in AAA gained him the International League Most Valuable Player and Rookie of the Year. He led the International league with .354 batting average, .435 OBP, and .601 slugging percentage. He was traded in December 2014 to the Tampa Bay Rays.

For his amazing catch, Souza was awarded the MLB.com Greatness in Baseball Yearly (GIBBY) award for Play of the Year.

ZEROES–MAD MAX SCHERZER
TWO NO-HITTERS IN 2015–

June 20 vs the Pirates—at Nationals Park

- *A perfect game going into the 9th:* One strike away from a perfect game, after retiring 26 batters, Pirate Jose Tabata got hit by a pitch either via a misplaced slider or the batter's misplaced elbow….just one strike away from the 22nd perfect game in history.

- *106 pitches, 82 for strikes*—mostly fastballs in the upper 90s. Scherzer's 16 strikeouts were a career high and set a Nationals team record.

- Scherzer's previous outing was a complete game, and he became the 5th pitcher in history to allow one hit or fewer in two consecutive games, drawing comparisons with Johnny Vander Meer (Reds) who pitched back to back no-hitters in 1938.

October 4 vs the Mets—at Citi Field

- *109 pitches*—104 game score (2nd only to Kerry Wood's 105 game score with his twenty-strikeout game with the Cubs vs Astros in 1998)

- The only base runner came on an error by Yunel Escobar (2B).

- *17 Strikeouts* (a new Nats record): Scherzer tied Nolan Ryan for the most strikeouts in a no-hitter. It was the 52nd seventeen strikeout game in MLB history.

- *9 Consecutive Strikeouts:* coming after the error by Escobar. The MLB record is 10 consecutive strikeouts (Tom Seaver Mets 1970)

- *0 walks*—reached a three ball count just twice

- Scherzer also out hit the Mets with a single off of Matt Harvey.

- Described by some as one of the best, most dominant, games ever pitched

Notable:

- Wilson Ramos was the catcher for all three Nationals no-hitters.

- With two no-hitters in one season, Scherzer joins a club with Johnny Vander Meer (1938 Reds), Allie Reynolds (1951 Yankees), Virgil Trucks (1952 Tigers), Nolan Ryan (1973 Angels), and Roy Halladay (2010 Phillies).

ZEROES—SHUTOUTS:

LEADERS EACH SEASON

Jordan Zimmermann leads with 4 total, Max Scherzer with 3 (see highlights)

2005	1	John Patterson RHP
2006	1	Pedro Astacio RHP
2007	0	
2008	0	
2009	1	John Lannan LHP
2010	1	Livan Hernandez RHP
2011	2	Livan Hernandez RHP, Jason Marquis RHP
2012	1	Gio Gonzalez LHP
2013	4	**Jordan Zimmermann (2) RHP,** Stephen Strasburg RHP, Gio Gonzalez LHP
2014	4	**Jordan Zimmermann (2) RHP,** Tanner Roark RHP, Doug Fister RHP
2015	3	**Max Scherzer RHP (3)**

ZEROES—Team SHUTOUTS

How Many Times the Nats SHUTOUT Their Opponent (how many shutouts did #1 have) and how many times they were shutout).

Year	Nats Shutouts	League Leader	Nats Shutout by Opponent
2005	9	Cardinals (14)	11
2006	3	Tigers (16)	8
2007	6	Padres (20)	12
2008	8	Red Sox (16)	21
2009	3	Giants (18)	7
2010	5	Phillies (21)	14
2011	10	Phillies (21)	14
2012	9	Angels (16)	8
2013	13	Dodgers (22)	12
2014	19	Cardinals (23)	8
2015	13	Dodger/Cubs (21)	12

The two ZIMMERMAN-N's

According to Wikipedia, the name "Zimmerman" derives from the German last name "Zimmermann" which means carpenter. It is the 441st most common surname in the U.S. (Zimmer=room, mann=man or worker).

Home

- **Ryan:** Born September 28, 1984—Washington, NC

- **Jordan:** Born May 23, 1986—Auburndale, WI

College

- **Ryan:** University of VA Cavaliers (starting shortstop)—NCAA Division I

- **Jordan:** University of Wisconsin Stevens Point (starting pitcher)—NCAA Division III

Drafted

- **Ryan:** 1st round, 4th overall pick, by the Nats in the 2005 MLB Draft
- **Jordan:** 2nd round, 67th pick, by the Nats in the 2007 MLB Draft

MLB Debut

- **Ryan:** September 1, 2005
- **Jordan:** April 20, 2009

All-Star

- **Ryan:** 1 time (2009)
- **Jordan:** 2 times (2013, 2014)

ZOOM: Bang ZOOM...

- Z is for "Bang, ZOOM, go the Fireworks," and "Bang, ZOOM, another curly 'W' is in the books!"

- *Charlie Sloes*—Signature Slogans—lead play by play radio man—with the Nats since February 24, 2005.

- As Charlie relates it, Bang! Zoom! Started during the ten game winning streak in 2005 and the 20 6 month of June when there was a frenzy over the Nats' unexpected early success. The Curly "W" came about a week or so later. Charlie and then partner Dave Shea came up with the idea during a game, thinking about what to call a win—then decided to call all the wins like that. Sloes jokes that maybe he should have patented the two slogans! The Curly "W" symbol pretty much replaced the original D.C. logo. (nats320 blog)

About the Author

Ann came by her baseball roots naturally, having grown up in baseball crazy St. Louis. Her mom used to hang out at legendary Hall of Fame, then-Cardinals manager Branch Rickey's house (classmates with his daughter) and later taught Hall of Fame, Cardinals announcer Jack Buck's son, Joe. Plus, her sister lived next door to another legend, Cardinal Hall of Famer Stan Musial! The path to the Washington Nationals started when Ann transitioned from working for a hard rock radio station in L.A. (KWEST, now defunct) to a career with the CIA. She spent twenty-five years working as an operations officer, serving her country and seeing the world while enjoying a tremendously meaningful and exciting job.

Over time, Ann went from enjoying minor and major league games to reading a lot on the subject, with Yankee slugger Mickey Mantle and colorful Giants manager John McGraw being favorite topics. Staying up on rankings, stats, and records also came into play, and whipping out facts/stats with the guys at work (surprise!) proved entertaining. As all baseball fans know, you get hooked on it. For Ann, serving abroad seemed to amplify the connection with the sport that symbolizes America.

Returning from overseas, the family went to a lot of Potomac Nationals games (then known as the Cannons and Cardinals-affiliated), great fun for her son Mikey, who was five and only interested in collecting foul balls. Pitching phenom and future Nats outfielder Rick Ankiel was the hot topic in Woodbridge at that time. The Good family also went to the short-lived Maryland Fall Ball League (a little chilly), occasional games in Baltimore, and spring training (Grapefruit League), while cheering on Mikey in Little League. Youth baseball was serious stuff in Saudi Arabia.

The Washington Nationals arrived in 2005 and luckily they were back in Virginia with season tickets, assigned to section 320 at RFK where a number of baseball fans converged (remember the Nats320 blog).

Sometime in January 2015, Ann was checking out new/old baseball books to read, noted there were not many Nats titles yet, and (inexplicably) decided to write a book she would want to buy. Here is what resulted! She hopes the next version includes a new "W" entry: the first World Series win! Go Nats!

INDEX:

T

U

V

W

X

Y

Z

APPENDIX

Most of these numbers are from fangraphs.com – check them out for explanations of the various categories.

HITTERS:

BA (Batting Average):

3.40 Excellent
3.25 Great
3.00 Above Average
2.75 Average
2.50 Below Average
2.25 Poor
2.00 Awful

OBP (On Base Percentage):

0.390 Excellent
0.370 Great
0.340 Above Average
0.320 Average
0.310 Below Average
0.300 Poor
0.290 Awful

SLG (Slugging Percentage):

.600 Excellent
.550 Great
.450 Above Average
.400 Average
.360 Below Average
.300 Poor
.260 Awful

OPS (On Base plus Slugging Percentage):

1.000 Excellent
.900 Great
.800 Above Average
.710 Average
.670 Below Average
.600 Poor
.570 Awful

ISO (Isolated Power) – a measure of hitter's raw power and frequency of extra base hits

0.250 Excellent
0.200 Great
0.170 Above Average
0.140 Average
0.120 Below Average
0.100 Poor
0.080 Awful

WAR (Wins Above Replacement) for Position Players and Pitchers:

Stat measures a player's total value/contributions to the team (if the player gets injured, and was replaced by a minor league or low level bench player, how much value would the team be losing?):

0.1 Scrub
1-2 Role Player
2-3 Solid Starter
3-4 Good Player
4-5 All-Star
5-6 Superstar
6+ MVP

wRC & wRC+ (Weighted Runs Created and Weighted Runs Created Plus):

wRC is an estimate of the number of runs created by a player; wRC+ makes adjustments for ballpark and factors in the league average.

wRC		wRC+
105	160	*Excellent*
90	140	*Great*
75	115	*Above Average*
65	100	*Average*
60	80	*Below Average*
50	75	*Poor*
40	60	*Awful*

wOBA (Weighted On Base Average):

wOBA captures the value of all of a hitter's contributions, using a "linear weights" approach assigning coefficients to every contribution dividing by plate appearances.

.400 Excellent
.370 Great
.340 Above Average
.320 Average
.310 Below Average
.300 Poor
.290 Awful

wRAA (Weighted Runs Above Average):

This stat measures the number of offensive runs a player contributes to their team compared to the average player; zero is league average.

40 Excellent
20 Great
10 Above Average
0 Average
-5 Below Average
-10 Poor
-20 Awful

PITCHERS

ERA (Earned Run Average - Starting Pitcher):

2.50 Excellent
3.00 Great
3.40 Above Average
3.75 Average
4.00 Below Average
4.30 Poor
4.60 Awful

FIP (Field Independent Pitching):

FIP is an estimate of a pitcher's run prevention independent of their defense performance.

2.90 Excellent
3.20 Great
3.50 Above Average
3.80 Average
4.10 Below Average